Ste
Diana Ross II

Further diaries of a Football Nobody

David McVay

REID PUBLISHING

A CIP catalogue record for this title is available from the British Library.

ISBN: 978-0-9926811-3-5

Typeset and design by Andrew Searle

Published by Reid Publishing

Printed and bound in India

Dedicated to Debby

For Tom and Jess. The pain gradually diminishes.
The sense of loss never relents. All my love. Always

In Memory of John Mounteney (1933-2014):
Family man. Notts County man. Lovely man.

Special thankyou:

Billy Ivory for his interest, advice and invaluable encouragement, the eternal optimist that is an essential part of being a raving Notts County fan

Mike Berry, *BACKPASS* owner, for unsurpassed research skills into retro football and his friendship.

Many thanks for reference and illustrations:

Paul Nathan and Mark Whiting

Cover points: Wendy Ackers and Mike Berry

INTRODUCTION

DURING my first two years as a sports journalist for the Nottingham Evening Post I managed to do something for Notts County that not even six years of blood, sweat and toil as a player could achieve. I guided them to two successive relegations.

It was not entirely my own fault. The players and management did their bit to transform Notts from a table-topping First Division side (two games into the 1983-84 season) into a team humbled 4-0 by Brentford in front of 3,857 fans at Meadow Lane in the Football League's third tier (March 4, 1986).

In that respect, I have always been indebted to Larry Lloyd during his brief but unsuccessful tenure at Meadow Lane. It was a time when many of my former team-mates were still active in the pro game, for Notts or elsewhere, so it was not uncommon for people to inquire about my current status as a journalist and why any semblance of a playing career was now at an end so relatively soon.

If Larry was in earshot, and strangely enough he seemed almost ubiquitous when that question was posed, before I could even muster a mumble of a lamentable excuse the answer would be provided by the current Notts manager: "Lack of ability. That's right isn't it David?"

Well, given Larry's glittering prizes gained primarily with Nottingham Forest, it was difficult to argue, and given his expanding girth and frame back then, it was also unwise.

It's probably one of the reasons for *Steak Diana Ross II*, some sort of purgative endeavour to remind myself that I could at least kick a football in a straight line. Now and again.

Oddly and sad to report, the more I re-read some of the notes I made during my last two seasons with the Magpies, the more I could see that Larry's pithy barb contained more than an element of truth.

There were, however, other reasons to write a sequel to a book that first appeared in print just over 13 years ago.

Billy Ivory, who scripted the play of the original book that ran for two weeks at the Nottingham Playhouse in 2012, has been encouraging me to bring out some sort of follow-up. His enthusiasm has rubbed off, even on me, and it will be a mighty relief to that beleaguered Notts fan that he no longer needs to fear another email dropping in his inbox seeking solace and advice.

Also another huge Notts supporter, Paul Mace, a fourth generation one at that, has written an expansive and impressive tome spanning six decades at Meadow Lane, tracing that history with his own thoughts and those of the players, managers and chairmen who shaped the past and ultimately the future of the club.

It would be nothing short of the truth to say that it compares favourably with Colin Slater's superb *Tied Up With Notts*, having been fortunate to be involved in the editing and publishing of both excellent books.

Since Meadow Lane is so redolent with definitive Notts County pages, the urge to write about the old club proved irresistible though the depth and range of subject matter in this particular publication scarcely comes close to the aforementioned titles.

Add the ingredient of that truly marvellous tribute to Jimmy Sirrel and Jack Wheeler, in the form of the statue that was unveiled in May adjacent to the ground, and the timing to pay further homage to that incomparable pairing could not be more apposite.

Unlike the first effort, there has not been the set of meticulous diaries that I kept as a fledging at Notts, rather odd jottings in a half-empty diary and sketches in notepads long buried beneath books and newspaper cuttings that evoke the spirit of that era.

As often occurs with the progression of years, the long-term recall can become more vivid, perhaps more rose-tinted, likely with a striped edging in black and white.

Happy days, not-so-happy days and downright miserable ones. Good or bad, thanks for helping with the memories, Larry.

1977

This was as good as it got as the 1977 season began. Isolated still life was fine but once on the move, the entire show went pear-shaped.

WHEN Jimmy Sirrel returned to Notts County in the winter of 1977 for his second managerial spell, Elvis recently had left the building, departed Graceland to Rock and Roll heaven by all accounts.

Back on earth in Nottingham, the Magpies were next to bottom of Division Two and in urgent need of firm leadership and a fair amount of luck to prevent a relegation to football's lower reaches. It was deep down in the basement section of the league tables where Sirrel had first encountered Notts when he was appointed manager eight years earlier and though there had been much progress on the pitch, Meadow Lane and the internal mechanisms remained largely the same aside from the natural recycling of playing personnel.

Training facilities were scarce and often randomly selected, sometimes at the 11th hour when the cold weather descended with its icy grip; Albert still mashed his sweet tea in the boiler room whose only nod to modern technology was a state-of-the-art wash tub and spin-dryer instead of the old manual mangle version.

And yet the winds of change were on the brink of blowing through the domestic game. In fact, some of the strongest gales were sweeping across the south bank of the River Trent where Brian Clough was once more trying to establish an East Midlands dynasty after an initial attempt had been thwarted by his own resignation from Derby County.

As that 1970s decade hurtled towards its conclusion, Britain would be welcoming its first £1million footballer and its first woman Prime Minister. Things could never be the same again.

In the beginning. The County team photo as the new 1977-78 season starts... and then (below) Jolly Jack manufactured the second coming. Jimmy and the Smurf replace Ronnie and Mick Jones in a mist-shrouded winter photo call to reflect the changes at the top…and bottom (see third from left back row).

October 1977

FUNNY how things work out. Is it a week? Or maybe just a day. Whatever the time span that is a long time in politics, football's equivalent seems to be a month. The last month to precise.

They hadn't exactly tied a ribbon, yellow or any shade of black and white for that matter, to welcome the prodigal back. But that was the way. When I was asked, no told, by County manager Ronnie Fenton that my interests were best served going for a loan spell elsewhere, they had scarcely splashed out on a farewell party either. Though Ronnie would have been delighted to put up some bunting and decorative banners expressing sentiments along the lines of Good Riddance or Don't Call Us displayed prominently above the sign marked exit at Meadow Lane. Just over a month ago it was.

Four games into the new season and without a first-team win and Elvis barely cold in his coffin but Ronnie would have picked the late, great Graceland legend, stiff, carrying extra lard and clearly not match fit, ahead of me.

Actually Martha, who washed and ironed the training kit in the boiler room, would have made the team sheet before McVay D, who, since the annual pre-season gruel and stamina training in around the verdant, sweaty and undulating hills of Colwick Woods, had spent the remainder of my time doing 'solitary'. Well the equivalent, honing my talent such as it was with the schoolboy triallists and part-time youth team coach whose common denominator was the level of skill each possessed….relatively none. But then as a 22-year-old has-been of inconsequential standing who couldn't even get his pick for the reserves, who was I to pass judgment let alone a football.

"Torquay United have shown an interest," Ronnie had told me gleefully early last month. Lincoln City, Peterborough United, anyone of a lower standing might have been interested for all I knew but geographically, sparing the expense of a long-haul flight to Sydney or a slow boat to China, this was as far as he could propel this outcast without attaching me to the barrel of a cannon and signing me up for Fred Karno's Circus as *Davido: The Human Torpedo*.

Then again, since Ronnie always felt that my football acumen was more suited for the Big Top, perhaps the Devon Riviera was, after all, second choice. Still, he could not contain his delight in telling this languid defender to take his leave along with *all* of his boots.

"What both pairs, the studs and moulded boss?" I asked, also assuming correctly that the train ticket to Torquay was of the one-way variety.

Dressing-room tales of the Devon Express filtered through my mind as the train chugged its way to the end of line, a journey of Ancient Mariner proportions to all stations that had survived the Beecham cuts as far as I could tell in the gathering gloom, Newton Abbot and beyond until the sound of gulls, or was it an albatross, woke me from slumber.

The Devon Express was an ironic way of relating the slow pace of life in the county and also how professional footballers who were transferred to that neck of the woods were destined to remain there, riding the ghostly train, unable to escape its magnetic spell, doomed forever to a life of clotted cream, knotted hankies and faux-pirate accents.

Torquay, Plymouth and next stop Exeter before a calling to the bar beckoned, landlord of the Stag and Thistle Dawlish, Topness or Exmouth. Like crew members on the Mary Celeste plotting a course through the Bermuda Triangle, passengers on the Devon Express simply disappeared off the radar.

Nearing the end of the line I was recalling Ronnie's first day in charge two years previously when Jimmy Sirrel had departed to try and save Sheffield United from relegation to the Second Division.

"I suppose we'll just carry on calling him Ronnie," I had told local radio when asked how things might change, or not, after our former reserve team coach replaced Jimmy as manager.

"Let's get one thing straight, from now on you call me Boss," began Ronnie's first-team talk at the helm 20 minutes after that fateful radio interview. One game later, after a 2-0 debut win for the new Boss, out I went, dropped. It went downhill from there.

Yet Torquay and their quaint Plainmoor ground was not the drudge that I had expected. The digs for starters, staying with a family whose 18-year-old son was an amateur with the Fourth Division side but whose overriding ambition was to study at Cambridge, the university not the club managed by Ron Atkinson.

My first revelation was a sort of Jerusalem moment when I discovered meals could be green and pleasant without requiring pre-chilled bog rolls on standby to assist consumption. Out of tourist season, Torquay held as much attraction as Belper on a bleak Tuesday night but that was not a bad thing.

Stripped of my trusty Ford Corsair whose sixth sense and two and a half legal tyres were locked into most of Nottingham's finest kebab and curry establishments and whose engine cut out within 50 feet of any public house, I was left to watch television and enjoy the occasional night out with new team-mates, an affable, friendly bunch but not in the County class of quaffers led admirably over the years by Billy Brindley and Brian Stubbs. Besides the keg beer was so appalling on the south coast, Badger bitter being the best of a bad lot, it was enough to drive a young man to sobriety.

There was also the little matter of football matches and September was a busy calendar month for Fourth Division clubs, eight games and a midweek fixture every week. Thus trips to Barnsley and Huddersfield meant an overnight stay the evening before, a coach ride home post-match, dropping off the Bristol contingent at Easton-in-Gordano services before heading home to Plainmoor in the wee small hours.

Such mornings tinged with bittersweet reminiscence, arriving home to the chink of the early sunlight and the clink of the milkman's delivery…normally a sight and sound that brought me out in a cold sweat, what with the impending hangover yet to kick in before training or the bedside stranger, in all shapes and sizes, that had to be kicked out of bed...or left behind.

This was indeed rehabilitation in so many ways.

Away from nautical musings on the south coast back in Nottingham, my old muckers were steering an alternative course which was heading for the rocks, a sinking feeling that would spell the end, quite literally, for the ill-fated captain Fenton of the good ship County.

After a trouncing at Fulham, it emerged that some of the squad had been out in a club called the Arriba on Thursday night, engaging in soda-syphon fights with local councillors or other pseudo dignitaries. A rogue cockney called Martyn Busby, signed from QPR, Pedro Richards, a Meadows lad who was brought up in a remote Basque village and diminutive Dave Smith, the former apprentice whose preferred reading matter was *Fiesta Readers' Wives* during nursery school, were confirmed among the usual suspects as well as Eric Probert, a dark, moody talented midfield player who drained beer glasses faster than County's Golden Girl ticket sellers dropped their knickers. That was lightning quick.

As results worsened, no wins in six League games, Ronnie got to hear of the misdemeanour and punished the culprits with fines and omission from the next home game against Blackpool. Sadly, it provided the prelude to his downfall. The Centenary Club at County, underneath the Main Stand, had long been a thriving and ribald institution where players, press, privileged fans and some of the top brass gathered after a game to slug alcohol at an alarming rate of knots.

It was also the first port of call for many reserve players once the Saturday game had kicked off and they had shown their faces 'up top' in the stand for the obligatory 10 minutes.

In the Centenary Club, hosts and devoted supporters John and Pat Mehew displayed their drinks and bar prices on a small pock-holed blackboard with white stick-on letters. Pat and John also owned The Railway Inn, a pub in nearby Netherfield where licensing hours took a leaf out of British Rail's timetable for running trains. i.e. intolerably late. They were smashing folk but seldom paid attention to detail, especially when it came to their own bar price board.

I never did find out who re-arranged the legend that would help terminate Ronnie's days at Notts, though I had a fair idea about the identity of the literary giant.

The Arriba had come to my rescue many times before when all pubs and landlords had tired of my company. The sleaze-pot death trap on Bottle Lane was always an open invitation for an early morning nightcap, a hallucinatory haven induced by cheap spirits and cigar smoke while the Worthington E-sodden carpets inspired weevil-like qualities in revellers who wobbled but never fell down. A fortnight previously a soda-syphon shootout at the same venue had begun Ronnie's demise and now another unlikely source was to pave the way for my return.

Since 'Buzzer' Busby could speak only mockney, Pedro struggled with basic English grammar and Probey was just plain Tyke glum, their little sidekick seemed the logical villain. I surmised that the diminutive Smithy was tall enough to reach up behind the bar and snatch the drinks list away without Pat and John's knowledge, the pair being mostly as inebriated by the top shelf whisky as their customers.

Not being a Class A drinker, Smithy would have been sozzled enough himself by full-time to greet the gathering throng with a beaming smile and the new price list board. He was certainly old enough to remember television's *Beat the Clock* that was the finale to *Sunday Night at the London Palladium.*

Even the spelling was pretty straightforward. RONNIE FENTON IS... orange and pineapple juices, peanuts, lemon and lime, lemonade... simple enough. I even grasped that gin would play a vital part but as the visiting players, national and local press, designated fans and local business bigwigs and guests entered the Centenary Club after another listless County performance, just where did little Smudger get the second 'f' to beat the clock and complete the well-worn phrase... A FUCKING CUNT. Genius.

October 10

THE call had come after Torquay had vanquished Brentford 2-1 at the weekend, a month after I had been sent packing to Plainmoor. Mike Green, the engaging Torquay manager, told the local paper that he would pay Notts County £5,000 to secure my services.

"Jesus fucking christ David, you canne buy a fucking loaf of bread for that son. Get your boots and get back here," the unmistakable Jimmy Sirrel instructions were barked down the other end of the phone.

All four boots, I presumed rightly.

Following Smithy's word game and after a 4-1 midweek defeat away to Sheffield United, Ronnie had been sacked and Sirrel, recently departed manager of said Sheffield United, returned to Meadow Lane two years after leaving for Bramall Lane.

So *au revoir* Torquay and its palm tree promenades. *Bonjour* Meadow Lane and the farm fodder slaughter house across the road.

Funny how things work out.

October 14

JIMMY, unusually, is effusive. So much so that he has promoted me back to the first-team squad for training today. Stubbs, Richards, Eric McManus, Mick Vinter, the familiar faces welcome me back. Others were not so sure, Sammy Chapman signed from Forest in the summer is one but Busby, the syphon-gang leader, had departed back to whence he'd come just a few months earlier, to QPR for double the £40,000 Ronnie had paid the London club. Don Masson, David Needham and now Buzzer, the cash flow between club chairmen Jack Dunnett and Jim Gregory was well lubricated.

How Colin Addison must have rued Busby's leaving of Meadow Lane.

I remember the former Forest and Arsenal inside forward joining Notts just under a year ago as assistant manager, a breath of fresh air whose unquenchable desire to talk, rabbit on and on and on, even mid-coaching, was mitigated by the fact that he could really trap, control and pass a football like few of we lowly specimens in the Ressies (in my halcyon days before demotion to the schoolboys second XI) had ever encountered. The squad who knew him as Addo all agreed. He was a player and anyone or any pass that did not meet his level of satisfaction was dubbed 'Two Bob'. Addo was old school and old currency. One who could read the game. However, it was his inability to read a programme, actually the changes on a team sheet, that cost him his job at Notts.

Researching the value of one Martyn Busby at Highbury, Addison didn't realise that his surveillance target was not in the team and wrote a rather unfavourable report back from Arsenal on the poor unfortunate who had replaced him in the QPR team.

It was a mistake without doubt but the special relationship between chairmen Jack and Jim meant there would be no reprieve for one of the game's good guys.

October 25

"AYE David, I am putting you in charge of the reserves tomorrow night son," Jimmy told me this morning. "They are a young set of bodies, eh. They need a bit of leadership, you play centre-half and show them how it's done son."

Leaner, fitter and considerably more alcohol-free, my chest puffed out a few inches even at the prospect of the Old Show Ground on a dismal October night. Of course it turned out to be a filthy evening near the Humber but we salvaged a point with a late goal, sliding several yards on my backside in the sodden Scunny mud to nudge in for a 1-1 draw.

October 26

BACK in the old routine. A few shandies on the Wednesday day-off along with a snooker foursome at a club near Theatre Square in town.

"I have to be home to feed the dog in half an hour," Smithy had announced. Such were the responsibilities of the married man and dog owner.

"Meet in the Flying Horse if you and Pedro are up for it McVay, around 7.30 by the time I have serviced the bride and sorted the dogs out," he added. The fourth member of the potting crew was Tristan Benjamin, a fleet-of-foot young professional with an outstanding Afro haircut that had taken over his head and now had its expansionist locks trained on bringing Sneinton and neighbouring St Ann's to their knees.

But Benjy will not be there. His marriage vows were nurtured as seriously as his hair and he rarely ventured out on a lads' night out no matter what the day of the week.

However, being any day other than Thursday or Friday there was every chance that Richards, Smith, myself and probably a few of the older County lags would indeed be gathering at the Horse around 7ish.

October 27

THE session was not too punishing last night with luminaries such as Brindley (unavailable for selection, otherwise engaged with Gillingham Football Club) and Stubbs (otherwise engaged with the darts team at Royal British Legion Club, Keyworth) notable absentees. Besides I have extra lay-ins before reporting for training at 10am now. It's just over a year since I bought an upstairs maisonette in the 'Posh' Park, an upmarket residential area just a few minutes' walk from the city centre, the daily commute to Meadow Lane in Brindley's red Humber from Clifton via Beeston and his early morning egg round a thing of the past.

No regrets but I do miss the banter.

"Come on you fat bastard, get your socks on, eggs to deliver then I'll show you how to tackle you lazy sod." Brought a tear to the eye.

"It will be an investment David," brother Paul had told me upon purchase of £11,600. At the moment it's a millstone of bills, special Park levies and a cloying mortgage though the neighbours, like Ronnie before them, would be more than happy to assist, pay in full even, to accommodate a move for me as far away as possible from them.

October 28

RESTORATION back to the first-team squad had its reward although naturally, there were displacement casualties along the way. And some of the sick and wounded were a joyous sight to behold.

Brian Mitchell was a point in case, a tiny Scottish apprentice who, by means of listening to his incessant twaddle, envisaged himself somewhere between Jim Baxter and Denis Law as a player and Sean Connery and Rod Stewart as a sex symbol. In fact 'Titch', his obvious nickname, was more Andy Stewart as a sex symbol and his deceased Scottish Soldier as a player.

Even at a summer pre-season training camp under Ronnie's regime, at the private Oakham school in Leicestershire, Titch thought himself leader of the pack. After an inaugural school greeting from Headmaster Fenton conveying the need for fitness, avoiding the ample local pubs, not to fraternise with the locals, especially the ample local women and their ample assets, and keep a low profile among the community, the lower sixth were dismissed and allowed out of the school gates to buy provisions from the Oakham tuck shops.

A swift glance into the tap room of the nearest public house, just yards outside the school gates, revealed the 16-year-old Titch with a pint in one hand and cigarette in the other. It was 12.30pm on the first day of term. If that did not endear him to the senior pros, his increasingly sneering attitude on my slippery slope to isolation then

Torquay was bloody infuriating for this former first-team regular.

"You smug little bastard," I once informed him one day when, as his *coup de grace*, he shoved my boots back in my face and told me to 'clean your own fucken boots cos ya nay gonna be fucken needen them in this club any longer…sonny!'

Since murdering apprentices was still a hanging offence according to English football law, I bit my lip and headed to Torquay. But it was worth it. Unsurprisingly while Titch flourished under Ronnie, it did not take Sirrel long to suss out a fellow Scot as less than the genuine article.

Watching Mitchell carry the huge kit hamper into the dressing room at the Old Show Ground the previous Tuesday night induced a pleasurably dark inner feeling that I knew was wrong and should have been guilt-laden… but it wasn't. The playboy of the western world and isles was now kitman for the Ressies at Scunthorpe, diligently laying out the shirts, shorts and socks.

"Hope the boots are spotless Titch," I opined while reaching up for the No.4 black and white striped shirt and casting an eye of undisguised contempt on the boot boy.

November 1

PROGRESS in the Anglo-Scottish Cup had been one of Ronnie Fenton's parting gifts, one that Jimmy grasped willingly. Still, didn't expect to return so swiftly to the first-team even if this was one of those so-called 'Mickey Mouse' competitions. It was wise never to mention it in those terms to Jimmy, however, because travelling up to play St Mirren the day before the game, our manager was going 'home', his disposition improving with every mile travelled north up the M6.

"Will ya take a luke at that vyou, Jackson, eh?" he beamed, indicating a panorama just north of Penrith to our physio Jack Wheeler sitting on the coach's front seat across from him. "Yes boss," Jack's response was on auto-pilot but the truth was that the nearer the border loomed, the more Sirrel's accent, indecipherable at the best of times, became positively alien.

Unfortunately his mission in Paisley to beat Alex Ferguson's side was not as spectacular as the scenery.

Just before half-time we lose a one-nil first leg advantage in the semi-final tie and it was then we notice that one corner of the ground is illuminated by a floodlight that once graced the land of Subbuteo table soccer. Running to retrieve a long ball, the stadium was suddenly plunged into darkness and as we fumbled about as if playing a game of blindman's bluff, the St Mirren forwards trot merrily away with the ball after a pre-match diet of carrots and night vision goggles.

Well that was my excuse for a desperate foul in the 18-yard area, the penalty mercifully spurned by Frank McGarvey, who atones for the glaring error by scoring the winner in the first half of extra-time.

In the quaint but warm clubhouse, there were bagpipes and pipers and all manner of Scottish greetings for victors and vanquished alike, whisky, haggis and more. Sirrel was subdued but having iterated in the dressing room that we must have just ONE pint to be sociable then back on the bus, it is when several of the squad accepted the bar steward's kind invitation for a second round of drinks that the man from the Gorbals saw the red mist.

"Jesus fucking christ, what the fuck did I tell you!" he stood gripping the back of the seats at the front of the coach after he had herded every single one of us onto the bus without allowing anyone to savour even a drop of the second pint.

Geoff Skeritt, County's long-suffering bus driver, had turned on the engine and the heaters in an attempt to defrost the atmosphere. It didn't work.

"Youz are a disgrace to the club and to me tonight," Sirrel snarled, almost foaming at the mouth, apoplectic at what he considered a personal slight on his home turf. "You will not embarrass me or this football club like that ever again. Geoffrey, let's get back to the fucking hotel. Pronto sunshine eh!"

A Scotsman in exile despises losing to the English but being beaten by another Scot runs a close second…and we had perpetrated that cardinal sin with a hapless display on and off the Love Street pitch.

November 3

JIMMY'S practice matches remain a Thursday burden for all, made more irksome when the little apprentice Gordon Mair, playing in the reserves, tries to take a lump out of my leg. Must be a Scottish midget mafia thing.

"Kick the little runt back McBay," Pedro urges quite sensibly.

"Little boys should be seen not heard, eh Mitch," the offending Jocks skulking back to defensive duties. That told them. Though Stubbs and Chapman clearly thought the Pedro method, pioneered by Bob Worthington, was the best remedy for apprentice impudence.

November 5

AFTER the fireworks of the other night in Scotland, Jimmy, typically, had mellowed and focuses on the real job in hand, saving Notts from relegation to Division Three. Brighton and Hove Albion are the next team to stand in the way of his objective.

His return to Meadow Lane has so far reaped the first two league wins of the season. And optimism.

My own revival continues mainly because Jimmy has his favourites list, those who he thinks are right for the task ahead. He also has his out-of-favour favourites list.

As well as Mitchell, little Smithy is another destined gradually to adapt to the North Midlands League routine of midweek trips to Halifax, Scunthorpe, Hull and Barnsley Reserves. Vertically challenged players are not for Jimmy's taste, besides after Smithy once asked for compassionate leave on the grounds that his dog had been run over outside his Sherwood house, the boss has never been quite certain of his agenda since.

Instead, he relies on his old and not-so-old contemptibles; McManus is a class act in goal, Pedro and Ray O'Brien as good as it gets as full-backs. Stubbs has lost David Needham to QPR the previous season replaced by the granite veteran Chapman for company at centre-half. And when Alan Birchenall, a Nottingham-raised football nomad, returned from America to join Notts the previous month, I did some basic calculations. Mathematics was never my strongest subject but I estimated that the diamond threesome at the central hub of defence boasted a total age of 959 years. That figure went above the millennium mark when Les Bradd was added. The Romans had not lasted as long in England. There were also Sirrel veterans Steve Carter and Arthur Mann but since the latter was fitter, stronger and faster than most of the teenagers on the County books, that was a step in the right direction away from euthanasia. And of course, I was back in an uncomfortable right midfield role.

Christ, we don't have a chance! Panic set in studying first me then the rest of the home team dressing room before the Brighton game.

What I didn't realise, and what Jimmy already knew, was that at this Second Division level, older and more accomplished heads could make up for legs less sprightly and lost yardage.

And even though Brighton are fancied for promotion, especially with Alan Mullery in charge, they are no match for Dad's Army and their willing volunteers. There is even a Pike on the bench, a young Paul Hooks, whose sending-off three minutes after arriving as a substitute in the season's opener for kicking a Blackburn Rovers defender confirmed the folly of his youth. Still, 'stupid boy' was not the expression that came readily to Ronnie Fenton's mind or lips in the post-match analysis that day.

There is no repeat this afternoon. The match is buzzing with atmosphere, the ground crisp, the weather sunny and as I close on Brian Horton, a sliding tackle takes the

Brighton hard man off by the knees and into the shale running track just in front of the dugouts, prone in pain in the horizontal position.

"Jesus! That felt good," my best tackle for two and a half years at Meadow Lane; the only decent one I have ever made, Brindley, a masterclass in rock-hard clobbering, would argue. "He won't be getting up from that in a hurry."

And then ten minutes later, midway through the first half.

"Christ! That fucking hurt." Horton, now vertical, happily for him, exacts revenge.

No matter. After relentless pressure, Chapman punts a ball high into the penalty area with a minute remaining and the Vint's curiously permed blond locks, arrested, as they should have been, in a hirsute time warp in 1971 Boston, get a touch and a back header that brings two points and a third win on the bounce.

Later that Saturday Night
The Ford Corsair Mark II

ANOTHER of Jimmy's discoveries had also departed Meadow Lane shortly after my return. Ian Scanlon, Scan the Man or Scanny, catapulted to fame by securing a hat-trick in two seconds or thereabouts against Sheffield Wednesday in the not too dim and distant past only for his scoring acumen to falter after Sirrel's departure to Bramall Lane. Thereafter, an increasingly fractious relationship developed with Ronnie.

It reached its nadir when he travelled to Carlisle for a festive game only to be told he was dropped. The free-scoring winger then made history by becoming the first Scottish footballer to travel north of Hadrian's Wall seeking sanctuary and gainful employment before announcing his intention to wed a wealthy heiress, having, he claimed, inherited a small fortune himself from a recently deceased relative.

Eventually Scanlon called a truce with Ronnie though he was never the same player again and he has left to join Aberdeen. His credibility was never the same either. Turned out there was no inheritance and his betrothed was a vicar's daughter from Wilford, a quasi-village on the south bank of the Trent.

Apart from that lightning hat-trick, Scanny's legacy was a compatriot and mate in the motor trade called Vic who rented a garage in an art deco building in the centre of West Bridgford. Vic was a good mechanic but his sense of vision in seeing a mug coming over a mile away was a talent to be envied.

Really I should have known better after the first 'motor' purchased from Vic's Vehicular Market.

"Aye, I've put a 1300 Morris engine in it so it should go like dung off a pitchfork, so it should," Vic explained when presenting me with a black Mini Cooper. Black in the sense that it was daubed in dull black masonry paint reserved for exterior toilet walls, probably layered on with a trowel, and a Mini Cooper in the sense that neither doors actually fitted and there was a disconcerting hole just below the accelerator, brake and clutch pedals.

Despite that obvious lack of bodyweight and its reportedly turbo-charged engine, the Mini struggled to get up even the slightest of gradients without being overhauled by sympathetic Lada and Skoda drivers. It was when water started to flood into the driver's side during winter forays through exceedingly long and deep puddles that I was obliged to 'trade' it in.

Vic's replacement was a green Ford Corsair, possibly camouflage green since the day it was manufactured lay somewhere between the Second World War and the Vietnam War.

It was a brute of a car and of course Vic had to plunge something into its bowels to make it work.

"Aye, just a gear box and transmission. The old one's knackered and I canne get it sorted till I get a winch big enough and strong enough to lift the thing up and out and bodge…aye replace it with the new second-hand one."

So it was in celebration of victory that I chauffeured Pedro and Smithy around Nottingham in the green machine and its mystery transmission box on Bonfire Night.

Following the inevitable cocktail of lager and lager in the Centenary Club, we make our way to the old 'Queers' Bar' situated at the rear of the Flying Horse, one of several glass-fronted or sectioned-off drinking areas in the city's famous old pub.

"Not much going on here," complains Smithy after a glug of lager with a dash of blackcurrant.

"Well there won't be for you in this bar will there Smudger?" Pedro replies, observing Smith's tidgy right digit upraised from his pint of lager and blackcurrant (his familiar drinking style). "Though if you keep ordering that drink and holding your little finger like that...well the night is young after all." Cue infectious cackling laugh.

"Upstairs, come on let's see who's in," the errant digit decides.

Around 8pm and the city throbs to its latest arrivals from the suburbs, busloads from the south and Clifton at Broad Marsh, from the northern wilderness of Mansfield at the Victoria Centre and then the fearsome coachloads that had breached border controls and escaped from Strelley and Ilkeston to assault Mount Street bus station just to the west of Maid Marian Way.

The Wild Women of Wonga were refined debutantes in comparison to the clientele that clambered from those charabancs on a Saturday night. And somewhere amongst their ranks was a native squaw running loose with Smithy's name on her spear.

A raucous crowd in the top bar included Paul Hammond, a local lad playing for Crystal Palace in goal, but none of the County team, all the married lads off home or back to their own local pubs by now.

Since the Forest side held sway almost exclusively in the trendy Uriah Heep wine bar, there was no likelihood of our two camps even remotely meeting up until disco fever beckoned at Isabellas or Annabelles around midnight.

In the meantime, Hammond was on good form as we made our way down Clumber Street from the Old Corner Pin to the Lion via a pub called the Crystal Palace.

"They named it in your honour Hammond."

"I can see that, the barmaid's forgot to take her ugly pills and she keeps dropping glasses."

"And her tits are nearly as big as yours."

In the Fountain on Bridlesmith Gate there was a whiff of something in the Nottingham air, the aroma of new money that complemented the new suits, new wine bars, new shops and boutiques. There was also the whiff of Smithy, sneaking from the direction of the gent's toilets with a huge, beaming grin on his face.

"He's pissed in your pint glass in the bogs, Hammond."

"I fucking know that. He can't help himself, one of these days someone is going to drink it and give him a right good hiding, the dirty little sod."

Time to go.

"99?" It was Pedro. Clearly he had unfinished business with a wench there. The Wild Women of Wonga and Mansfield miners' wives would have to wait for Smithy another Saturday night.

Sunday Morning
The Ford Corsair Mark II (discontinued)

DESPITE a raft of nightclubs opening in and around the city centre, the 99 still attracted a faithful following on the south bank of the river, what with the nearby Trent Bridge arches offering *al fresco* shagging no matter how inclement the weather.

The old, old crowd! Christ! Even Torquay in January has got to be better than this. The faces were all too familiar. Doug Fraser, the former Forest player now manager of somewhere or other. Amazing Grace, the good time had by all, her friends Spotted Dick (if she spotted dick, she had it) and the big woman who could have been a bloke but nobody could pluck up the courage to ask. It all added up to Cold Gossip, as some wag had declared when sizing up a dance floor awash with the present calibre of disco diva.

Then a Forest director's daughter or was it a farmer's daughter? Couldn't recall the name but rumour had it she was taking over from Grace, like the incoming window cleaner buys the appointments book off the departing shammy leather man.

Her polishing act, French or otherwise, was apparently very good though she had not toted her bucket and ladders over to the cricketing fraternity. As yet, that was.

She and Grace compared notes in the little black book of the retiring Godmother, a gift to the new Don Giovanni. Pages of names on team sheets with the added bonus of marks out of ten.

Put one way, if the Forest midfield was being rated in the *Sunday People*, few would merit star man or even average man while one of the back four would have failed, in cricketing parlance, to trouble the scorers.

"Come on, let's get out of here," Smithy was told.

"Not likely mate, I've pulled."

He was right. And it was not even his own todger either. To prove it, he swivelled round mimicking Les Dawson's Cosmo Smallpiece with hands firmly grasping the breasts of one of Grace's friends, not one from the inner circle, or coven as most preferred it. It could have been Short Fat Sally or Tubby Teresa, both of whom bore a striking resemblance to one another in the dimly lit shadows of clubs like the 99, which funnily enough they mainly frequented after dark.

They were a bizarre bunch of women all told, this nomadic tribe who materialised unerringly wherever professional sportsmen were socialising after hours and who defied, no reversed, Boils Law of Increasing Beer Returns that defines the more lager consumed, the more desirable women appeared.

The Ten-to-Twos, the Twenty-past-Twos and the Half-past-Nevers. That was how they had been categorised by Smithy during a slack night at the 99 some time ago, figures relating to the 2 o'clock in the morning closing time and the deadline when each one of them might fully expect to leave the premises with a member of the opposite sex. Many, it seemed, veered towards the Half-past-Nevers section when choosing their specialist subject.

But now as Smithy laid his head where his hands were groping, I began to feel sick and left. Pedro spotted my departure and, having as much joy with one of the coven as the Brighton left-winger had in getting past him earlier that day, joined me on the footpath leading to the parked Corsair.

"Where to Robin?"

"The Batcave. Or better Mr Miller's. Still be open, still time to pull. Women, not swimming McBay eh?"

Pedro's basic English had improved since he arrived a decade ago in the Meadows area of Nottingham from the Basque village of Laguardia where he was raised by his grandmother. But he still had the odd problem with pronunciation.

"OK. Let's go for it."

The thing with the Ford Corsair, I often reflected, was that sturdy and robust as it was, it seldom obeyed the normal fundamental rules of gravity and road holding that more modern cars had grasped.

For example, taking corners or sharp bends were particularly eventful motoring moments, the driver never quite sure that even though the front half of the Corsair was pointing in the right direction and had safely negotiated the manoeuvre, the rear end would follow.

A pantomime horse in equine turmoil.

So trundling up a deserted London Road from the 99 club was not much of a strain for the Corsair. But half a mile nearer town at Sam Ward's island, named after the owner of the petrol station on its northern side of the huge roundabout, the route became a little trickier, not really improved by a frost that was rapidly gripping and an alcohol-fuelled driver convinced he was James Hunt in a strangely unconvincing green McLaren.

Accordingly, I managed to get the front of the Corsair beyond the petrol station landmark but as the road inclined upwards toward the ten-pin bowling alley and the Lace Market and Mr Miller's, the hind legs could not keep pace and stubbornly called it a day. The recalcitrant rear end dragged men and machine across the icy road, up and over the pavement before landing nose first on a piece of wasteland that doubled for a car park during daylight hours.

The force and heavyweight Corsair had smashed through a metal barrier attached about waist high to concrete posts acting as a perimeter for the temporary parking bays.

With engine running I sneaked a tentative view behind to assess status and dissolved into *Star Trek* speak.

Damage report Mr Scott?

Not good Captain. The engines canna take it.

Shit, that was all I needed, another fucking Scottish accent telling me how fucking bad I was in my darkest hour. The dilithium crystals might be OK but the rest was crap news.

Somehow, one of the metal bars had smashed through the back window directly behind the front seats and blasted open the rear passenger door.

"Why the fuck didn't Smithy get in the back?" I remember thinking looking over at the passenger seat for signs of life. I needn't have fretted.

Having been flung back then hurled to the floor on impact, Pedro gradually crawled back into his leather seat.

"Fucking hell man, you could have killed me. Are you fucking nuts or something?"

"Would definitely have killed Smithy if he hadn't pulled," I was still cursing my bad luck. "Tubby Theresa saved his life tonight."

"Fucking hell man. What the fucking hell. You could have fucking killed me. Hey?"

Whatever his shortcomings in the English language, when it came to basic guttural blaspheming Pedro had more than mastered the idiom as well as the pronunciation.

Trying to ignore that I might have also been killed, I opened my own door and looked around. No police sirens. So far, so good. Dislodging the metal bar that had wedged in the broken glass of the window and the opposite door panel was the next task accomplished.

Getting off the main drag was now a priority and into the Lace Market that offered pitch blackness and plenty of open spaces to park up.

As Pedro repeated his allegation for a third time, I noticed the gate was locked. Fortunately the Corsair had bludgeoned a nice gap between two concrete pillars.

The rear door would not close fully so, as I pointed the beast out of the car park by way of the path we had just entered seconds previously, I calmly asked Pedro to shut the fuck up mate, turn around and kindly keep the door closed manually.

A minute later, we had made it to another equally deserted and barren wasteland near St Mary's Church, turned off the engine and considered tactics.

"I'm off McBay. You're a fucking maniac man. I need to get home in one piece. See you Monday."

So much for Plan A.

Did he know that I once had Viv Anderson sitting in that exact same seat and admiring the view of the Park not so long ago. Before he became famous of course. As Lennon might have put it, when he wasn't even the best right-back in Nottingham. Pedro was. *Tempus fugit* and so had Pedro.

My alcohol-addled logic truly thought this an ungrateful act from someone whose life I had just saved with, quite frankly, the speed and reflexes of James Hunt.

Those same pickled brain cells also worked out that if I stretched my left hand far enough behind and across I could keep the back door shut while driving with one hand in the second gear to which Vic's novel transmission box now appeared permanently cemented. Plan B.

How I made it back to my flat in the Park I could not recall when I awoke later that day.

Or how had I managed to reverse it into the bloody garage, the end one of a row of five hardly big enough to accommodate Vic's holey Mini let alone this ancient blob of the road. All I recalled was not wanting the neighbours to see the dented Corsair, because given the physical and mental scars I had inflicted on that small cul-de-sac of maisonette dwellers in the Park over the past 12 months or so, they would have rejoiced to see the battered remains of Ford's finest. And probably informed the police for good measure.

In the shaded confines of the garage, sweating gin from an increasingly furrowed and sledgehammered brow, another thought flashed across the brain during damage viewing.

What sort of fiendish transplant could Vic perform now to fix this bloody mess?

November 12

TURF Moor; Planet Earth; 3.22pm; "Jesus, NASA could use your right foot to launch their rockets McVay," was Birchenall's aside after I had ballooned an early chance high over the bar and stands into the firmament towards Nelson, his column not the nearby parish.

"Thought you were in California not Florida smart arse," I countered lamely.

"San Jose Earthquakes son. And that's where your fucking shot's ending up."

"Has it gone into orbit yet, Rocky?" Chapman queried as I retreated shoulders slumped back to a midfield berth. The nickname derived from my rendition of a Beatles song on the *White Album* rather than pugilist tendencies and that last attempt to hit the target could have been described as a haymaker.

That was another thing about old pros. Their legs might be going but their grey matter in the art of ridicule was, if anything, getting acutely, painfully sharper.

A thunderstorm of biblical magnitude sweeping over the East Lancashire terrain was also ominous. Still it could not return my unguided missile. Steve Kindon and Paul Fletcher put Burnley two up and the game was over. Back to the drawing board for management; shooting practice for the players, me in particular.

November 14

NOT on parade in the dressing room this morning is Glan Letheren, on loan from Leeds, who has returned to Elland Road. For a Welsh goalkeeper he seems to hold more crosses than he drops but he was only here as cover for Eric Mac. That and to prove he is the worst tipster this side of the Severn Bridge, a sequence of seven bets in one month without a single return. Can't figure out who are the mugs but it's not George Aitken, who apart from the swanky Vic Club has a string of betting shops to assist less affluent punters to part with their hard-earned cash, or in our case not so hard-earned. The Taff Letheren departs without playing a game but reminds me on leaving of a goal I scored past him at Scunthorpe. Such is the shuttered world of the football fraternity. I could remember the goal, my first that counted at the other end without actually requiring the aid of a deflection from an alien spacecraft or human limb, but had no idea who was supposed to be keeping it out. A League Cup tie at the Old Show Ground. Was this betting scam some sort of payback? Hard to fathom the way of the Druids.

November 28

YOU can take the boy out of the pubs, but ….they were coming back to haunt me, the watering holes, dens of iniquity or any establishment that could describe itself as licensed premises in a five-mile radius.

That month's sabbatical in Torquay, refraining from heavy supping, smoking and stuffing the face with highly spiced exotic food, undoubtedly had been kind to my body, digestive system and domestic cistern in terms of hygiene and the purchase of industrial strength cleaning fluids. But it had not proven to be addictive. Quite the reverse.

And since Nottingham was awash with landlords and pubs more than happy to extend a warm and grateful welcome to the prodigal far in excess of his employers, I was seldom short of a public bar in which to relax and sniff any passing barmaid's apron.

The two that held the most magnetic appeal, at least to the Corsair before it committed hara-kiri on a metallic pole earlier this month, were the Loggerheads and the Newmarket. The former was a refuge for dodgy characters, the latter for dodgy haircuts. Tough choice. The Loggers was closer to my working environment and from 6pm each evening was invaded by every member of the nearby Railway Arches community, legions of refrigeration experts, car mechanics and bodywork sprayers and repairers, who filled those premises on the fringes of the Broad Marsh bus station and shopping centre, a vulgar monstrosity that had been erected on the demolished remains of the city's most ancient thoroughfares and landmarks.

Since Vic was having problems with the kamikaze Corsair, I was moving in the right circles and a white Mark II Ford Cortina, unlockable but reliable, had been purchased for £100 as the next shagless wagon to ferry me about the provinces. It was provided by Sprayer Ron, Dream-On Dixie and Big Al, the trio who comprised a happy band of car body builders and repairers who also happened to be Notts County fans to a man.

To the front of the Loggers was a row of houses on Cliff Road and a useful pedestrian rat run through to the News House pub and Canal Street and freedom in case Plod paid an unwanted visit to some of the meaner streaks in the tap room. That is if Plod could identify anyone through the wall of tobacco smoke that blockaded said tap room from 6pm onwards.

If the Black Plague planned a comeback performance in Nottingham, the considered opinion was that it would swerve the Loggerheads for fear of contracting some fatal disease.

Below ran Nottingham's famous caves while to the rear, a vertiginous cliff wall edged up to the old County Court on High Pavement where Buster Edwards, the Great Train Spotter, was sentenced after a brief appearance over a decade previously.

Still further back when people were hanged for sneezing incorrectly in the market place, it had been a debtor's prison where those miscreants unable to afford to pay were dangled by the neck, or worse, over the side as punishment for being poor and broke or atishooing through the wrong nostril.

Luckily the invention of large settees and sofas spared latter-day residents from Bulwell to Clifton a similar fate, allowing the underprivileged to seek shelter behind the luxuriant fabrics when the rent woman or tick man came knocking on the door to collect monies due.

Half a mile up the road from the scene of the Corsair calamity stood the Newmarket, a haven not only for hair disasters but also their victims, mostly CAMRA (Campaign for Real Ale) devotees and undergraduates, predominantly female on a Monday night when student discounts applied in city centre clubs.

However, any association with the CAMRA crowd ruled a dalliance with any young member of the opposite sex impossible. The only hope was that if Wednesday's Grab-a-Granny night at the Palais could become the main weekly attraction following Grab-a-Geek night across the road on Mondays.

Still, who in their right mind would take a chance on a variety of oddities who narrowly failed to make the final audition for the *Star Wars* bar? Among them pot-bellied, pot-holed of face Ginger Jeff, hair shading not gender blending, and his Bobby Charlton in reverse, the more he combed his few remaining strands forward, the more bald his entire head became.

Somewhere in between these two bastions of lowlife, the Arriba beckoned as virtually the last resort, that title being reserved for Uriah Heep, 50 yards away down

Fletcher Gate and home to the chinking white wine Frascati and Liebfraumilch set where no beer-blooded drinking man would set foot. More so for those of a black-and-white-striped persuasion since amongst its privileged winos were Nottingham Forest's First Division high fliers.

"When is that fucking bubble gonna burst?" little Smithy was asking one Monday night. Having lost to Leeds then only managed a 0-0 draw at home to West Brom at the weekend, Clough's youngish upstarts remained a point ahead of Everton on top of the table.

"Bloody Bob bloody Wilson's fault," chimed up Tony Green, ardent Notts fan and Newmarket landlord, from behind the bar. He was also a former bobby on the beat now nicknamed Frankenstein because of the surgical bolts in his neck that kept his head from falling off after being left for dead in a ditch following a horrific car crash in a previous life.

There was tragedy somewhere in that mangled wreck but it never surfaced. For now, his head and brain wobbled on against all the odds and gravitational pull while standing defiant in the face of decimal coinage, barring customers willy-nilly who could not muster a sixpenny piece or threepenny bit as part payment for a pint.

Madness was not essential but producing a certificate of insanity usually expedited entrance to the Newmarket on even the busiest of nights.

"The thing is Greeny we just need to concentrate on us, not them," I was arguing tamely. Since Sirrel's return as manager, we had steadily moved out of the relegation places and a 0-0 draw at Millwall's Cold Blow Lane on Saturday was another point in the right direction.

"When's the crumpet coming in Greeny?" Smithy moved the conversation on to one of his favourite topics.

His audience was Benjamin and Lloyd Richards, two handsome young pros whose rare presence was down to the reserve game being called off at the Lane that night. In black leather trench coats and carrying the menacing scowls of thwarted Ressies, Shaft had arrived in the Newmarket. Minding Charlie 'Smithy' Drake with his ridiculous perm at the bar. Only the blackcurrant top in the half lagers and the occasional flashing smile from the pair gave the game away.

"Benjy, Lloydy where are we heading my men?" Smithy affected some Pidgin Rasta in the manner of Jack Smethurst in *Love Thy Neighbour*.

"What kind of rasclat you lucking for man?" Smithy's fifth pint would be his last as he started to slur his impressions.

Benjamin and Lloyd were suitably amused, Greeny suitably bemused. Anything beyond colonial English was alien to him. Ginger Jeff disturbed a tuft on his head to display a fetching scabby skull laced with attractive puce pimples. In the corner, a group of female freshers had seen enough.

"Schladies, schladies, wudcha like to join us at the Arriba later on darlings? Come on m'ducks, let me weigh them shings, they sheem very heavy m'dear." Smithy's patter and perm inspired panic. The young girls, already shuffling to the exit, vanished in seconds.

My heart sank.

"I don't know how you do it. I really don't."

"Itch the way I tell 'em."

"Well fucking try telling 'em a different way you randy little sod."

Benjamin and Lloyd were now doubled up with laughter. Another night of sterile chat and sticky carpets awaited at the Arriba.

****

After negotiating the winding flights of stairs up to the dimly lit first floor of the Arriba, Smith and Benjamin made for the bar. Rum and cokes for Shaft and friends, gin and tonics for the male honkeys who watched middle-to-old-aged female honkeys dancing around handbags on the small dance floor wedged into the club's claustrophobic environs.

The next stage was two steps up to the middle section wherein the intelligentsia resided...that is those beyond the capacity to talk, think or stand but glad to sit down amongst like-minded individuals.

Two narrow staircases, stripped from the escape hatches of a Lancaster Bomber, led to the real dance floor and another bar at the top of the club. A soda syphon with a yellow sticker marked: 'In case of Fire, top up Whiskey First' summed up the staff and customer priorities. An old fireman's axe hanging on the wall of the middle bar labelled: 'Fire Exit' completed the safety drill for emergencies.

Luckily, the place was filling up quite nicely so in the event of arson or a late bonfire night, there would be plenty of charred bodies to protect regulars from the flames.

"Make it a sherbert David," announced one of the newcomers, Alan Birchenall, ambling to the bar where I was leaning heavily.

"What?"

"OK a Brucie."

"Pardon."

"Bruce Forsyth."

"Come again."

"Not on your nelly mate, or anywhere else," he laughed uncontrollably to a silent audience.

"Forsyth. Saga. Lager. David, come on now."

"You're making it up as you go along Birch."

"No strict cockney rhyming slang rules. God rest me soul me old cocker."

"But you were brought up in Hucknall, south of Mansfield, north of Ilkeston."

"A man moves on from his roots Davie boy. When you travel you'll realise."

From Nottingham to Chelsea via Sheffield did not sound convincing enough proof for a person to turn cockney but then who could fail not to have a soft spot for the North Notts East Ender.

The night dragged on. Smithy needed to fall down but the quagmire carpet drenched in his own gin and tonics and several 'Brucies' would not allow it. Instead he made the best of his upright position trying simultaneously to touch himself up and any women foolish enough to get within groping distance.

"Let's weigh 'em darling. Come on not many of them to the pound ma duck." It was hopeless, he was hopeless.

Eventually he joined the intelligentsia at level two.

Over in a dark corner, actually everywhere even with lights on was as dark as air raid curtains though some nooks and crannies were darker than others, and in one of those someone was chatting up a gorilla. On closer inspection, it turned out to be Brian Kilcline, the 6ft 4in slab of concrete and Notts County apprentice footballer of Meadow Lane.

"Killer, lad, you shouldn't be out this late son."

"You should talk Rocky."

"Yeh but I haven't got to clean out Jimmy's bathwater as my first task in the morning."

"I'll be fine," replied the bulk and drained a pint of disgusting Worthington E.

"Fancy another?"

"Save your money kid. Later."

As he trotted off, the floor shook beneath his steps. A cross between Desperate Dan and Mighty Joe Young and just turned 16, few people argued with 'Killer' despite his teenage status. If he could learn to control and head a football, he had a future in the game away from the travelling circus.

Once he kept the bench warm for Brian Clough's Derby in a European Cup semi-final against Juventus. But then John Sims boarded the Devon Express at a tender age and has never been seen since apart from unconfirmed sightings on rolling grassy knolls.

December 12

SOMETHING of a bad homecoming for the Birch on Saturday, losing 2-0 at the Palace, one of his many, many old clubs.

The pace might have diminished but his ability to name drop, from Bobby Moore to George Best and Pele, was world class and recently he had donated a San Jose Earthquakes t-shirt to prevent Jimmy from ordering me from the dinner table during Friday evening meals before away games.

"Aye that's fucking better," Sirrel had announced before food the other week at South Mimm's when I appeared wearing clean jeans, shoes and socks and that pressed white t-shirt with an obtrusive logo the size of Giant Haystacks. "About time you started to smarten yourself up David, eh? You were a bloody disgrace to my club last time. That won't happen again, eh son."

No Boss. Neither beard nor Army and Navy Stores second-hand t-shirts escape your notice. The most garish option always found favour with Jimmy though it had to be noted that he seemed to have kicked, licked or whatever, his tomato sauce bottle-licking habit at meal times. Unless like all addicts he had become more cunning in disguising it.

Maybe Tony Currie and some of their older pros had advised him on matters of etiquette at Sheffield United. Whatever the reason, the expectations before sitting down to eat had disappeared. Like Brindley's egg round, gone but not forgotten and truly missed.

December 15

"YER man across the water, eh! He's fucking everywhere eh Jackson! Television, newspapers, every fucking where, eh!" Jimmy Sirrel was regaling Jack Wheeler with his estimation of Brian Clough as the first-team prepared for training. Another full-scale practice match.

"Aye, well good luck to the boy, eh! We'll know soon enough, eh Jackson, we'll know soon enough."

"Yes boss," the ever-dutiful reply to such unfathomable musings.

Burnley visit tomorrow and I have a nostalgic pang glancing around the Thursday morning dressing room. Gone are Brindley, Probert has called it a day as did Scanny, no millionairess, just a pub to manage up north. Even Busby, the grating cockney, was a character of sorts. Gone too are the long lost red-hot spoon duels, cocks exposed and silverware warmed to boiling point by Albert's mashed mushy tea.

Characters, old-fashioned fun. And the inevitable mini-brawl. I miss them…though not the burn scars on the nob-end oddly enough.

December 16

JIMMY gets the old Corona bottle tops out. If he has mellowed a little, changed a bit here and there since returning from a chastening two years at Bramall Lane, some things have stayed the same. Including those endless practice matches, the last one finishing 5-4 to the reserves at about 12.15pm yesterday.

But instead of picking out the blue tops that represent County, he is going through the yellow team.

"Aye, this boy, at right-back, he canne turn if you run at him son," Sirrel with Paul Hooks in his line of vision.

"The two centre halves, Michael," he looks up pointedly at Mick Vinter. "They canne run eh! Canne run, the pair of them."

Having dismissed former England full-back Keith Newton as past his sell-by-date and Jim Thompson and Billy Rodaway as sub-standard defenders, Jimmy moves on.

"Aye and these two Brian and Samuel," Stubbs and Chapman, not exactly the quickest pairing in the Second Division, are on red alert. "They will not want to know after 20 minutes. Eh, Brian?"

"Yes boss," Stubbs happily chirps up knowing full well what his role, ably accompanied by Chapman, would be in the preceding 20 minutes to induce disinterest in Paul Fletcher and Steve Kindon. By any means possible, within or without the laws.

"And Alan, aye Birch," Sirrel has that glint in his eye as he carefully picks up and caresses a yellow bottle top. "They tell me you are some sort of vet-er-an, eh son?"

"So they say boss," Birch laughs.

"Well I have news for you son, eh. This fucking one's even fucking older than you. And he's got even less hair," the manager unable to control his chuckling. It is not his usual style to bring up the opposition so prominently. It might also have been cruel to dismiss such a respected professional like Peter Noble. Yet deep down Sirrel knew that every single one of the aforementioned Burnley team, even stranded as they were at the bottom of the league, was capable of beating anyone in the division on their day. As they had, just a few weeks previously when we failed to turn up at Turf Moor.

"Jesus christ Jackson, these boys are ready for it. Take them for a chuke up on the pitch Jackson, 20 minutes and away. Let them get settled on tomorrow eh!"

December 17

IT took only 14 minutes for disaffection to blight the Burnley ranks when Hooks headed in the first goal. By half-time Vinter had taken advantage of some sloppy defending and an own goal from Thompson totted up to 3-0, the final score. Jimmy's predictions had been eerily accurate in every way. The losers remained stranded bottom, six places behind us. Things are looking up for the Magpies.

At Forest, they are looking down. Having battered Manchester United 4-0 at Old Trafford, and Tony Woodcock scoring twice, Clough's team are still in pole position.

Jack had written out all the Saturday results and posted them on the notice board, adjacent the mirror that hung above the dilapidated electric fireplace. Sirrel was combing his hair on reflection.

"Aye Jackson, yer man across the fucking water eh!" we could hear Jimmy muttering as we departed the otherwise joyful dressing room on our way to the Centenary Club bar and Saturday night oblivion.

December 25

CHUKE-UP at the track and then back to the flat to collect a few things. An alcohol-free Christmas night in the Posthouse near Bolton. Two years ago in London, Frankie Lane, our resident reserve goalkeeper and first-team Scouser, smuggled in the Party 7s amongst his Mitre gloves, Pedro chinked the bottles of Bacardi and rum in his holdall. The cans of Skol and Kestrel lager were down to me. *Butch Cassidy and the Sundance Kid* made their television debuts but while ever there was a hole in the wall gang or in his own backside, Frankie was never going to appear in one of Ronnie Fenton's teams. We all thought that then however when he did, a few months later, Ronnie could not forgive him for a mistake that cost Frankie his Notts career. Probably why goalkeepers have to be a tad mad in this precarious profession.

We never did see the end of the film nor the bottle of rum despite some valiant efforts to polish off the lot. Green of gills or pallid of Party 7s, none of us saw much of the game the following day either, a 3-2 defeat at Fulham. For good measure, I didn't see much of the game at home to Oldham two days later even though I have it on good authority that I was playing, present on the pitch anyway, for more than half of it. Ronnie was miffed by Probert and Brindley for poor defending late on and gave me and Pedro the nod as we boarded the bus in west London after that Boxing Day defeat at Craven Cottage. I was ecstatic, elated. So much so, I threw up at Watford Gap and Leicester Forest East in celebration on the way home. Still, we did win 5-1. Allegedly.

December 26

WHEN I was but a lad in the sixth form at Fairham Comprehensive, my presence was requested several times by Everton for trials. Playing in the reserves alongside the likes of Jimmy Husband, a flying winger of Cup final and League title fame, Dai Davies, the Welsh goalkeeper and Henry Newton, a Forest and Derby legend and truly inspiring comfort for this awe-struck schoolboy, was a real privilege. Playing against Bolton Wanderers and a similarly-aged beast of a centre-half called Sam Allardyce was not. Even at left-back, I felt intimidated every time he approached the halfway line, still about 30 yards distant.

Today, he was eight yards away when he scored Bolton's first goal from a corner, his header taking a bit of Stubbs' skull with it as he barged it into the net. Note to self: he's not got any smaller over the intervening years. With Pedro injured I am at right-back and enjoying it even though we lose 2-0. They are top of the league and with nearly 25,000 crammed into Burnden Park and players like Peter Reid, Frank Worthington, Tony Dunne and Ray Train, you can see why. Sober reflection all round on the journey back. Not a sick bag or vomit-stop to be seen or had.

December 27

RAY O'Brien 2, Hull City 1. Our Irish full-back launches two left-foot shots from distance and the Christmas bonus comes late but just in time for some serious lock-in revelry at the Newmarket where the landlord Frankenstein Green is even accepting post-decimalisation era currency in return for best bitter. Of course he is pissed, drunk on Home Ales and a home win.

December 31

THE entire festive season has played havoc with social arrangements. "Any more of this and we'll have to take a vote on a winter break David lad," Stubbs announces with a pint in hand and a fag on the go in the Centenary Club after beating Bristol Rovers, me backing away from the smoke and beer fumes. "I mean, a bloke's got to have a drink and a smoke sometime over Christmas. But mind you David, you look after yourself. Keep fit, there's some big games coming up son," he adds, finishing another pint and drawing deep on the Woodbine.

'Bomber' Bradd (2) and young Hooks have ensured we are still unbeaten at home since Jimmy returned with a 3-2 win and more money to pay the mortgage. What did I do with it all before buying the flat in the Park and a transmission and gear-guzzling relic of a Corsair. "Responsibilities, David," an old friend, now a former friend, had once pointed out. Never that keen on responsibilities.

1978

January 2

HERO of the hour on New Year's Eve, stupid boy Pike two days later. Hooks blobs a penalty-kick straight at the Blackburn goalkeeper with ten minutes left and then Keith Fear heads an undeserved winner shortly after. "Stay on your feet, Rocky," O'Brien tells me afterwards. He's right. Still filling in for Pedro at right-back, a little eager and a bit green, I should have jockeyed and not dived in on their player who then crossed for the only goal of the game. It was Gordon Taylor. Bastard.

January 3

TWO days off! Time for a clean-up at the flat. I could have let the two girls who originally shared it with me do it, but they had long gone. I had thought it would be *Man About the House* nirvana, myself as Robin's Nest and two not-so-dopey girls stumbling from one hilarious scrape to another. That was the idea when I invited them, at very little cost, to share a bedroom that doubled for an airing cupboard. Sorted. Turned out Delia's heroines were Germaine Greer and Boedecia while Roz, the quiet one, might have been a secret admirer of Lucrezia Borgia for all I knew. I did know her less-than-secret admirer was a part-time gyspy and full-time dickhead who used the balcony as a monkey swings up trees as an alternative form of entrance to the flat's front door. He was also fond of jumping off Gunthorpe Bridge into the fast flowing River Trent below for Saturday night japes. That and downing the odd bottle of bleach in one swig. Neither of which had the desired effect, desired by me, of doing for the blighter.

Of course they had to go. Clough's managerial career at Leeds lasted longer though on the odd windy night I swear I can still hear the sound of a Domestos-fuelled didicoy hanging on to the balcony rails above the rustling leaves of the Park's overladen foliage fallout.

And how that bloody bleach would come in handy today.

The G Plan furniture from our Clifton council house dominates the front room. In fact it's the only furniture save for an old settee and chair Jason King threw out of

Department S on the grounds of bad taste. An upturned carboard box that passes for a dining table adorned with the most recent newspaper available providing a tablecloth completes the ambience. Estate agents and potential buyers please note.

The one and half bedrooms are damp and bedraggled by even damper clothes because since the day the flat was sold, the Servowarm central heating system has done everything bar work or heat the flat. Neither Serves nor Warms but trying to get hold of one of their repair men is to go in search of Lord Lucan or rocking horse manure.

Grilling sausage sarnies in the kitchen is a better way of survival and cheaper source of heat in deepest winter rather than a dietary option. The other is homemade sweet and sour sauce to put on the sausages but after a girl called Donna (surname unknown) from the Newmarket hurled the recently-consumed house speciality out of the French windows onto the balcony during what should have been something of a flat-warming ceremony, the sweet and sour has generally been off the menu.

She insisted it was the grub. Not the sight of me naked. Not seen her since.

January 4

THE sausages are off this morning. So am I. Spent last night with Pedro, Smithy and Brindley, on a guest appearance on leave from the Gills of Kent, traipsing from the Newmarket to the Palais, Mr Miller's and Scamps. From the bottom to the tips really. And the Cortina was not even stolen. It had been pinched in the past two consecutive months, first from outside the Loggerheads then the Rancliffe Arms in Bunny where Alan Hill, the former Forest goalkeeper, is landlord. Gave me and a few mates a lift home in his white Jag, all the way to the Park. Nice car, nice bloke. Sadly the Cortina was found the following day in Coalville and Anstey respectively. Hoped for a hat-trick and an insurance pay-out but parked outside the Newmarket with keys in the ignition failed to attract any joy or riders.

January 5

DRIVE to Clifton where Pat (mum) and aunty Peggy are down and short of cash. Tell me about it. Apart from the usual costs of 'owning' a house, residents in the Park Estate pay an extra charge to the Oxford University Chest because they live in an estate that they own. Just as well the Chest didn't buy Clifton Estate, they'd have to hire the SPG* rejects to collect the taxes. Thinking of renting a bench in the Park, could be cheaper. And warmer.

But going back to that house where Granddad and Grandmother spent their final days, a yearning ache for winter mornings in warm bunk beds with a family together and cooked breakfasts and homemade gingerbread. And running upstairs to pray that JFK would live and then praying in the same room 12 years later to the same empty space that Granddad would survive. What a first class twat I was.

Christ McVay. Get a grip. And a drink.

Gin and Nick Drake, *Northern Sky*, followed by *Your Move* and then Wishbone Ash back at the flat. They reckon punk is all the rage. Like County v Oldham a couple of years ago, the whole shooting match has passed me by.

* SPG was the Special Patrol Group, a notoriously violent unit of the Police Force based in London. Not to be confused with SIG which was Captain Scarlet's action stations phrase Spectrum is Green in the eponymous puppet show.

January 7

THE FA Cup distracts from our league position. I stay on my feet at right-back and a 2-1 win at Charlton results. Vinter gets a couple, O'Brien pulls a hamstring. I hesitate to give advice to our Irish defender. Jimmy, beaming in the dressing room afterwards, reckons we were down to seven fit men by the final whistle.

"It was a struggle eh, Jackson but these boys were up for a battle today. I sensed it Jackson."

He forgot to add his sense of desperation.

Things were so bad he selected little Smithy to start. Which was a bit like Ronnie picking me and Frankie Lane in the same team. Next port of call: International Rescue or the Samaritans.

January 8

SOMEWHERE north of Ripley and not far from the M1 was where John Sims could be found. Allegedly, because on a mission to take him home for a change of shirt before a charity game at Alfreton this afternoon, our convoy of three cars ends up on a mystery tour of D. H. Lawrence country and its many inviting pubs with the local lad as pilot and tour guide. For some reason Brindley is on board and he, Smithy, Sims, Pedro and myself arrive several pints late for kick-off and make no impression on the game whatsoever for 45 minutes. Not quite true. Brindley has been concentrating on bolstering his immunity to Skol lager, already considerable. He is outstanding on the right-wing. With their twin perms Smithy and Sims are Shirley Temple meets one of the Beverley Sisters. "You were brilliant Ped," Brindley tells his right-back. "McVay, you played like the celebrity comedian. Hilarious but nobody knew who you were. Hopeless." Fortunately, Jimmy's radar does not extend north of Ripley on Sunday afternoons. We hope.

January 14

AND he hasn't even bothered to thank me. I suppose that's gratitude. Crammed with what Jimmy would label 'all fancy dans but who can all play eh' Tottenham Hotspur, top of the table and don't they know it, arrive today and by half-time are just about on their way home. 3-1 down, two from Braddy and Vinter has forced one under Barry Daines. Pedro returns at full-back so all is well in defence and Simsy, normally up front and a confirmed leader of the line and at the bar, has dropped into central midfield and the two of us, with Flash Carter and Archie Mann, are just about keeping Hoddle, Perryman and Pratt quiet.

It ends 3-3. Should have held on is the general opinion. Perhaps class told. Colin Lee headed the first leveller for them. A few months ago he scored two on his last game for Torquay. It was my last game as well and I am certain I made one and a half of them against Brentford. The following week, Lee was hoisted shoulder-high at White Hart Lane by Spurs teammates after bagging four on his debut against Bristol Rovers. Tottenham had paid £60,000 after his two-goal display at Plainmoor. The 'loaf of bread' was back across the road from the Cattle Market. Certain the thankyou card must be in the post from north London soon.

January 16

APART from the alarming expense, moving to the Park has other drawbacks. Most of the indigenous population. Estate agents, solicitors and teachers and all manner of odious professionals. Including one footballer, though only vaguely professional with frequent lapses and not odious at all. Add frustrated traffic wardens and there is a potential top ten for the list come the revolution.

So you travel the wrong way around one of those huge, empty traffic islands at the top of the estate near Newcastle Drive just to save tyre fatigue to post a letter and suddenly two cars swoop in a pincer movement to prevent further progress like the Sweeney. Of course the Jaeger polo necks and spanking new Rovers are no match for the dishevelled disgrace of a Cortina Mark II and its occupant. They slide aside and allow my forward, erroneous movement. Fuck you and up the revolution! One small, meaningless victory in the class war. The battle wages on!

That was this morning. Too early this morning.

Yesterday was spent recovering from one of the few attractions of living in the Park. Dave Bury. Or his hospitality. A mate of my brother Paul, he's small, perfectly formed and owns a house and balcony overlooking the Park tennis courts where Connors, Nastase and a few others have played in summers past.

Whereas my balcony takes in a view of several overgrown shrubs and the ugly backside of Lenton, his embraces the very heart of the Park; the super-duper exclusive squash club, the pristine grass tennis courts and the immaculate bowling green and HQ. From the middle-aged cradle to the grave in panoramic vision.

Paul may have his designs on a squash club membership among other things. I have designs on his booze cabinet which on Saturday night was truly hammered by myself and young Fish, occasional flat mate and Spurs fan who was celebrating his team's narrow escape earlier that day.

Far too many professionals calling me 'fat', 'sad' or 'just piss off' for my liking. They will have to be lined up against the wall before the firing squad, denied a last cigarette for all I care. As for Bury. He may well be too bright, wealthy and/or educated for the proletariat but what the hell, a revolutionary army marches best on its vodka and assorted spirits. Brother Bury it is.

January 30

STAYING down on the south coast after our FA Cup tie was called off on Saturday. Jimmy plans a coach trip to the seaside to relieve the boredom. We have a free day to spend anywhere but in a pub. Late for the coach back to the hotel, grab a taxi but no fine. During Ronnie's reign, certain I was paying chairman Jolly Jack's win bonuses with the amount of money deducted for being late, deservedly so as it happened. Can't think why I missed the bus back. Brighton on a wet Monday; Belper on a bleak Tuesday. Spot the difference.

January 31

MARK Lawrenson drops a ricket in the first minute and Vinter is in like Flint to finish from a tight angle. Pedro is in perpetual overlapping mode on a bog of a Goldstone Ground. We win 2-1 but it's not as tight as that. Home at last in the early hours. Flat fucking freezing.

February 4/11

GAMES called off. Rain and snow. Flat is now officially Ice Station Zebra. Fish has found a stray body to keep him warm elsewhere. Could be female. The latter avoid ISZ… with good reason. Running out of sausage sarnies. Must pay gas bill and ask Oxford University Chest if they have a charitable wing that donates clean, warm blankets to worthy causes

February 12

TRIP to Shepshed to see my sister Sue, announcing she is expecting a sibling for Natalie later in the year. The Delisle Arms offers only Shippos but it's cheap and her husband John serves well into the wee small hours. Crash out in the best room. Wander upstairs to the loos in the middle of the night and take a wrong turn, tumbling down into the pushchair and carry cot at the bottom of the tight staircase. Nothing broken, more a tackle from John Inman than Graeme Souness. The baby-to-be's head well and truly wetted if a little prematurely.

February 13

THERE is a price to pay for the games being called off. Laps, half-laps and more laps around the pitch. To cleanse the body of all the badness during the lull. Or as Wesley proclaims: "Clears the shit out of you doesn't it Flash?" laughing insufferably as his giant, loping strides glide him effortlessly, or so it appears, over the cinder track, eating up the yards and sweating gallons of 'shit' out of his system in the process. In contrast, Flash Carter's little legs can't take him along quick enough to keep pace with the pack, his ever-decreasing stride painful to watch, hence Braddy's caustic remark. The game's up for Flash and so is last night's Chinese. Chundering up egg-fried rice onto the Kop terracing. If he could only save the bean sprouts, perfect Regan's revolving head and take aim at the goalmouth it would clear some of the snow that has settled on the pitch. He is still in the prone position as we pass by on another lap, claiming it's something he ate. Jimmy is muttering and tutting from the home-team dugout where he is supervising the laps. He is like a troll demanding a toll to cross the bridge to Flash, who can't risk his wrath to reach the sanctuary of the dressing room. As we head off for another circuit towards the Meadow Lane end with Jimmy in pursuit to inject more pace into the run, Flash seizes his chance and avoids the boss by skipping over the railings and heading off in the direction of the top car park before a U-turn will take him back into the changing areas. He moves gingerly, the snow and his own hurling taking their toll. Unlike Jimmy Troll.

February 16

WITH no break in the weather Jimmy is aching for a reasonably-sized pitch upon which to stage a full-scale practice match.

Frozen pitches, snowbound goalmouths everywhere. Training sessions are 11th hour affairs as Jimmy rings round last resorts in the early mornings to find a suitable surface, anywhere, anyone who owed the club or him a favour. There were plenty of takers. Indoor five-a-side games at Carlton Forum and Nottingham University only served to compound the cabin fever.

There was some fresh air when we arrived at Hyson Green Boys Club one Thursday morning in the newly acquired four-year-old Ford Transit van.

Named after a type of tea and once one of the wealthier and genteel suburbs at the turn of the century, the 'Green' was now G for Ganja territory and an intimidating place after dark for those unacquainted with the patch.

The training venue was half open with a fair sized seven-a-side pitch covered over by a corrugated roof and a wooden fence surround but crucially it allowed Sirrel's whistle to rule over a practice game for 90 minutes or more.

Nearing the end, the match had attracted a score or so of local schoolboys, all colours, all either truants from school or a day off because of the bad weather. The smart money was on the former.

Spotting the spectators, Jimmy stopped proceedings and invited the fans onto the pitch.

"Aye laddy, you fancy joining in then son?" he picked on a lean black youngster with Tristan Benjamin-tribute mop hair, who nodded to confirm.

Within a minute, there were 20 young lads running around, kicking balls and taking on Stubbs, Bradd and Vinter while Sirrel refereed then played his favourite right-wing position, taunting and teasing the School Second XX to get the 'fucken ball offame eh son!'

Virtually impossible to liaise with through media channels, Jimmy had his own unique way of communicating. No doubt methods lost on Saatchi and Saatchi busily trying to install the Iron Lady into No.10, but his PR skills to appeal to people, common or otherwise, are second to none.

February 18

THE ice has thawed and the weather is warmer (except in this frigging flat). And a frosty and fierce reception (what else?) at Cold Blow Lane. County's first FA Cup fifth round tie for 23 years ends in an awful penalty decision against us and a 2-1 defeat. Jimmy is furious, ranting at the referee.

"A fucking cheat Jackson. My players have been cheated, Jesus fucking christ," is the recurring mantra in the dressing room with the Millwall fans baying for blood at some travelling supporters outside. Ugly place, ugly people.

A commiseration party in the TBI on Trent Bridge followed by more drinks in the Spread Eagle, the only pub in Nottingham that fills up after closing time. Just around the corner from Isabellas, it's a last watering hole for the desperate and thirsty before being forced to endure inflated nightclub bar prices. Pete Quilty, a County fan dubbed the singing landlord by himself, reopens the front door at 11.15pm and former and current County and Forest players pile in. And the Notts Fire Brigade from the City HQ just down the road on Shakespeare Street. Boat races and all drinking games are upstaged by the firefighters who demonstrate a knack of climbing under tables, up and over doors without spilling a drop with the sort of lithe acrobatics reserved for Romanian gymnasts of stunted growth or Chesty Morgan...whose growth is anything but stunted. No wonder the girls love a fireman in uniform and his trusty hosepipe. What chance the rest of us?

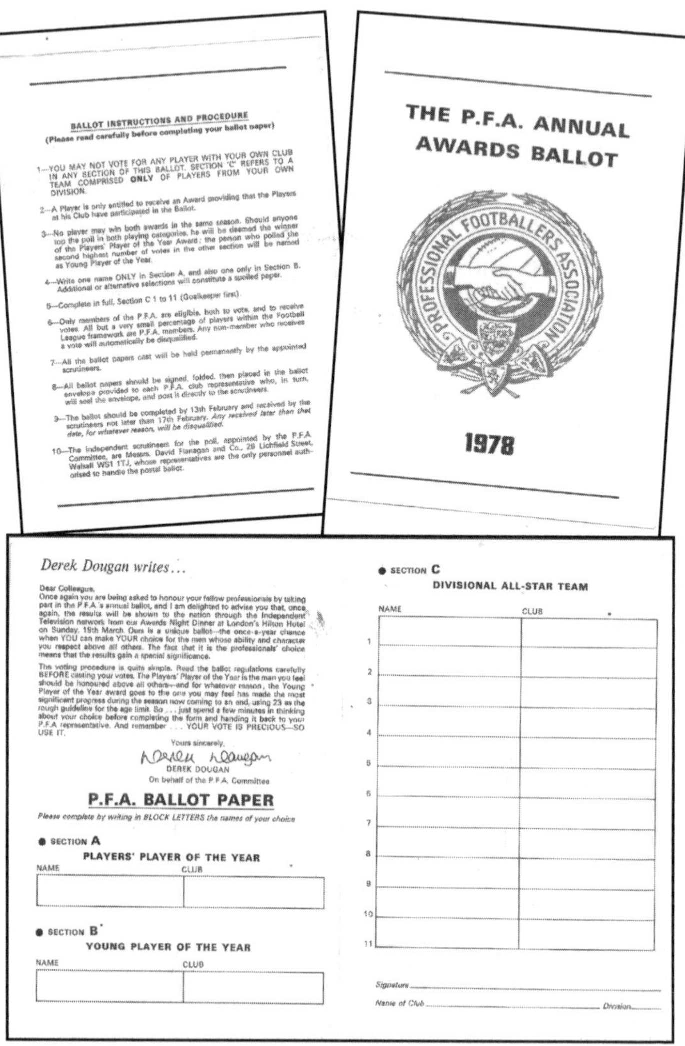

BALLOT INSTRUCTIONS AND PROCEDURE
(Please read carefully before completing your ballot paper)

1—YOU MAY NOT VOTE FOR ANY PLAYER WITH YOUR OWN CLUB IN ANY SECTION OF THIS BALLOT. SECTION 'C' REFERS TO A TEAM COMPRISED **ONLY** OF PLAYERS FROM YOUR OWN DIVISION.

2—A Player is only entitled to receive an Award providing that the Players at his Club have participated in the Ballot.

3—No player may win both awards in the same season. Should anyone top the poll in both playing categories, he will be deemed the winner of the Players' Player of the Year Award; the person who polled the second highest number of votes in the other section will be named as Young Player of the Year.

4—Write one name ONLY in Section A, and also one only in Section B. Additional or alternative selections will constitute a spoiled paper.

5—Complete in full, Section C 1 to 11 (Goalkeeper first).

6—Only members of the P.F.A. are eligible, both to vote, and to receive votes. All but a very small percentage of players within the Football League framework are P.F.A. members. Any non-member who receives a vote will automatically be disqualified.

7—All the ballot papers cast will be held permanently by the appointed scrutineers.

8—All ballot papers should be signed, folded, then placed in the ballot envelope provided to each P.F.A. club representative who, in turn, will seal the envelope, and post it directly to the scrutineers.

9—The ballot should be completed by 13th February and received by the scrutineers not later than 17th February. *Any received later than that date, for whatever reason, will be disqualified.*

10—The independent scrutineers for the poll, appointed by the P.F.A. Committee, are Messrs. David Flanagan and Co., 28 Lichfield Street, Walsall WS1 1TJ, whose representatives are the only personnel authorised to handle the postal ballot.

THE P.F.A. ANNUAL AWARDS BALLOT

1978

Derek Dougan writes...

Dear Colleague,
Once again you are being asked to honour your fellow professionals by taking part in the P.F.A.'s annual ballot, and I am delighted to advise you that, once again, the results will be shown to the nation through the Independent Television network from our Awards Night Dinner at London's Hilton Hotel on Sunday, 19th March. Ours is a unique ballot—the once-a-year chance when YOU can make YOUR choice for the men whose ability and character you respect above all others. The fact that it is the professionals' choice means that the results gain a special significance.

The voting procedure is quite simple. Read the ballot regulations carefully BEFORE casting your votes. The Players' Player of the Year is the man you feel should be honoured above all others—and for whatever reason, the Young Player of the Year award goes to the one you may feel has made the most significant progress during the season now coming to an end, using 23 as the rough guideline for the age limit. So . . . just spend a few minutes in thinking about your choice before completing the form and handing it back to your P.F.A representative. And remember . . . YOUR VOTE IS PRECIOUS—SO USE IT.

Yours sincerely,
Derek Dougan
DEREK DOUGAN
On behalf of the P.F.A. Committee

P.F.A. BALLOT PAPER

Please complete by writing in BLOCK LETTERS the names of your choice

● SECTION A
PLAYERS' PLAYER OF THE YEAR

NAME	CLUB

● SECTION B
YOUNG PLAYER OF THE YEAR

NAME	CLUB

● SECTION C
DIVISIONAL ALL-STAR TEAM

	NAME	CLUB
1		
2		
3		
4		
5		
6		
7		
8		
9		
10		
11		

Signature ....

Name of Club .... *Division* ....

Time was up for the PFA ballot form to decide the Player and Young Player of the year as well as the divisional award. The pristine paper speaks volumes for the enthusiasm of this voter.

February 19

SUNDAY in the Clifton Bridge Inn, with Chapman and assorted locals, remains a ritual worth the journey from the Park. Losing in the Cup means aggrieved County fans want a word and a scapegoat. Or both. But they have paid their money and though it may be hard work, it's warmer than the flat.

A real homestead pub nicknamed the Ponderosa after the ranch in *Bonanza*. The landlord, past or present, is called Cartwright. Or was it Little Joe and one of the barmaids looked like a Hoss? Who knew? Who cared? It was warm.

February 20

DISCOVER my PFA Player of the Year ballot sheet beneath the cardboard box table in the front room at the flat. Unlike my last general election paper, it remains blank. The same year as I voted for Jolly Jack (Lab), Norman Hunter won that inaugural award and I actually took the trouble to name a divisional team. Idiot on both counts. Still, even in February, the deadline has passed to make a choice despite our great leader Mr Dougan informing us that our vote is precious...so use it. Sorry Doogs, not that precious.

March 4

COLIN Murphy, the reserve team coach hired by Jimmy on his return to Meadow Lane, is in charge of the first XI at Brisbane Road. Jimmy is absent, on a mystery scouting mission so Killer tells us from the gaffer's diary that he reads in between sweeping out his office, an apprentice tradition handed down from Smithy and Pedro. Sadly no names of who he may be watching.

"Now listen Rocky, you gonna get over the halfway line and anywhere near the penalty area have a go son. OK? You got that my boy. Awwight, awwwight."

The Smurf has his arm around me on the team coach. The mockney accent and incessant diatribe are as irritating as the nervous blink, probably a legacy of his angst-ridden days as Derby County manager when the first-team players would lock him in the dressing room and bugger off to their Raynesway training ground without him.

His one-on-one team talk, inflicted on every player on the coach with the exception of Stubbs, Chapman and Birchenall who are old enough to know better, pays off. After 20 minutes I unleash a goal-bound right foot rasping shot that their goalkeeper John Jackson has difficulty grasping, doubled-up laughing as it bobbles reluctantly to the six-yard area where the ball, already on a go-slow, calls an all-out strike and downs tools. It gets worse. Far worse. I get even farther worse. It ends 0-0 at 90 minutes, about 89 minutes too long.

March 5

THE sun is out, the best birthday present. The flat is warm. I bathe in refracted sunlight in the lounge with toast on a cardboard box and Friday's *Nottingham Evening Post* collecting the crumbs of burnt bread and strawberry jam with fluffy bits where the bacteria lurks. What the hell, live dangerously as the flat thaws. Even Donna's hurled sweet and sour sausages have emerged in a flawless splat beneath layers of ice that have decorated the balcony for months. It looks like the preserved dung from a pre-historic beast. An archaeological dig is imminent.

March 11

THE ghosts of Christmas past return to haunt me this week. Tuesday night in Blackpool and Alan Groves, a mop-haired wayward left-winger, scores their second though Flash Carter is beamed down from his normal Martian mother ship when north of the Pennines and scores the leveller. Then today, his partner in crime at inside-left Les Chapman scores Oldham's second before Flash, now back in southerly climes and allowed to remain on planet earth by his Martian abductors, delivers our £80 win bonus with a late, late penalty. Groves and Chapman, Little and Large, the pair of jokers in unison on the left are one of the few things I can recall about that 5-1 thrashing on Boxing Day, a double act intent on extracting the Michael about my forward surges (usually without full control of the football) and backward defending (usually without full control of the body). They thought they were funny. In fact they probably were, much funnier than Little and Large. Definitely funnier than Mike and Bernie Winters. Just too inebriated, knackered and dizzy to notice.

March 21

A YOUNG lad named David Hunt signed from Derby for over £40,000 made his home debut against Mansfield tonight. In truth he is a good enough player but the dressing room felt, to a man, that with his pretty-boy looks his chosen career path should have been more in male modelling rather than as a muscular midfielder. Clearly neither was an option for me. Colin 'Foz' Foster, one of Mansfield's hard-as-nails defenders, welcomes Hunty to life in a Nottinghamshire derby with an almighty whack on the shins. Last season the Stags were aiming for promotion when their manager Peter Morris tried to sign me on a month's loan. Boy's a fool. A hamstring strain prevented the move. Fortunately for him. And Foz. They went up but while we are bad, Mansfield are terrible and remain rock bottom. Hunty's shins are swollen, black and blue but after a long and meaningful look in the mirror, it is obvious the face is intact and in pristine condition for the long night ahead. The real work now begins for our dreamboat midfielder. Not that I'm jealous mind you. Beware that green-eyed monster as my English Lit teacher taught me.

March 25

HOWEVER hard you get kicked up hill and down dale by Mansfield, there is nothing like a Billy Bremner tackle to refresh the parts other assassins fail to invigorate. A reminder of the good old days in the game when Brindley assisted wingers into nearby stands whereupon chairman Jolly Jack would pounce for his entrance fee, at best seat prices too. The ginger peril has already taken down Vinter and Flash before strafing my calves with his trademark calling card signed with six studs. They are near the bottom and Boothferry Park is, as always seems the case when we travel east to the Humber, in crumbling decay and in urgent need of a respectable crowd to fill the void on the vast empty terraces and stands. How does Bremner do it? Once of Leeds and Scotland, a Wembley-winning captain who has enthralled packed houses from Glasgow to Barcelona via Manchester and Munich. What drives him on in this barren waste on the frontiers of east Yorkshire, barely 6000 in the ground and most of them shouting abuse? And at him, because of his previous at Leeds. Only he knows, and when he levels the scores for a point that rekindles their survival hopes, it's as if he's just netted the winner at the Nou Camp in the European Cup final. And now my calf is really fucking throbbing as he celebrates in front of an ungrateful audience.

March 27

EASTER Monday. Allardyce and the Land of the Giants resurrected. Vinter, again, scores early on and a 1-1 draw with Bolton is progress. Definitely.

Today, this might be called an assist in some complicated stats system and increase my value considerably in the overall offensive pattern of play, inspiring gushing pundits to rave about a desire to keep the ball alive and wanting the game more. Back then it was a toe-poke back on a windy Easter Monday to Mick Vinter who made no mistake from two yards out. County 1, Bolton 0. It didn't last.

April 7

DROPPED for Millwall tomorrow. Can't blame the gaffer, pretty poor against Fulham on Tuesday night. On the plus side, there is new furniture in the kitchen at the maisonette. Having bought a washing machine that stopped work after the first cycle from Fast Eddy's second-hand shop on Alfreton Road, it is impossible to shift the thing out and down the stairs fully-laden as it is with a tubful of dirty water. Instead, a barrel of Home Bitter, 88 pints of Frankenstein's finest, sits neatly on top and allows the flow of real ale into the glass below and seals in the rancid smell trapped in the top loader from a bygone age of laundry mechanics. Even at three pints a day, it should last the month to FA Cup final day. Who am I kidding?

April 14

MET Brindley in the Maypole at Wilford. It's not a pole with strings attached parked in the middle of the village green around which gay schoolchildren and merry folk frolic and dance but a pub away from the main street next to a Co-op with as much rustic charm as Animal Farm. Maybe the circular shape compensates in some way to replicate the village fete attraction but that shape makes it very tricky trying to test personal sobriety, unable to bounce off walls as you are, shuffling around on some hellish cylindrical wall of death from Goose Fair until you stumble out the front door.

He's not in the side at Gillingham and with Jimmy and the first-team travelling up to Sunderland today a nostalgia-fest over several pints has been requested by both parties. By 2.30 in the afternoon the bar has shut but John Cuthbert, aka Cuff, proprietor of the nearby Talsta Hotel, knows not the meaning of last orders. A football fan who swings both ways, in purely football matters, though if pushed he is red and white deep down rather than our own black and white stripes. When he's not playing golf or driving a new Mercedes he's serving drinks behind the sort of 1960s hotel bar and restaurant that induces nausea even before a drink has passed the lips, plastic chairs to complement the flowers, wafer-thin paper napkins, bamboo fittings and Aussie antique dealers passing on their antipodean pearls of wisdom.

They buy vanloads of tat, the kind Family First and the Sally Army reject when clearing houses, then ship it by containers back to the motherland.

"What the fuck do we know about antiques? Nothing. But back home they know even fucking less," seems to be the general consensus from the two geezers from Sydney and Earls Court. They would have a field day at my flat, though maybe the G Plan is a little exclusive for their customers.

The beer is kegged Bass and dire but the bar is always open and Cuff indulges all-comers. Brindley is unhappy in Kent, so is his family. He wants to return, pack it in and get a 'proper job Macca'. I am shocked but he is not joking. More average Bass allows our minds to wander freely down Meadow and Memory Lane, Brindley's all-time best tackles, my all-time best albums, he's clueless on them all, before a final rendition of a Beatles medley and his swansong *Great Balls of Fire*. "The game's bent McVay. Game's gone, son," Brindley surmises while clinging on to his raised barstool. The weekend endeth here.

April 19

WEDNESDAY is Koo Kan night in the Loggerheads. Ten past six and the banter is in full flow. A pint reserved on the bar and a place in the card school by Malcolm Smith, fridge engineer and cold storage fitter extraordinaire. Who needed Uriah Heep or wine bars when a romantic night in playing Koo Kan and choking on Malc's fags lay in wait.

"Who you got Saturday McVay?" Smith inquired.

"Palace at home Malc and one we need to win."

"Well why they playing you?"

"Not really sure mate. Mind you, might not be playing anyway."

"Thank christ for that. Hear that everyone McVay's not playing on Saturday. Get a bet on a County win," Smith's cackle at his own jokes echoes around the tap room.

"And stop chucking queens away you stupid boy."

"Stop cheating and looking at my hand."

"Keep your hands up then."

"All you did in the war old man wasn't it?"

"Cheeky sod!"

The juke box warms up with Ned Miller's *From a Jack to a King*. It was going to be a long night. But I had come prepared. With £20 for gallons of ale and gallons of gin at the Arriba...not required as it happened.

April 20

TIMES are changing at the Lane. Birchenall has returned to America, Sims has joined Exeter and the Devon Express I so narrowly avoided. And suddenly without warning Jimmy invites me back into the first-team. From days trying to con a wage rise out of him, chastised for being unshaven for weeks and slovenly in dress to being hugged and lauded and defended in front of the senior pros, the Squirrel has something I can't explain. I will never get or understand it but will always respect it, even when mimicking him behind his back. This time, you really don't want to let the old sod down, do you McVay?

April 22

JIMMY is the ultimate blend of bullishness and caution.

"Aye nearly there, but not quite eh. Still work to be done youz boys, remember that."

Crystal Palace had been beaten 2-0, Vinter and Bradd prolific once more and I had been restored to midfield with Hunt. The beauty and the beast obviously but it was the old school mainly, McManus, Richards, O'Brien, Stubbs, Chapman, Carter and Mann.

And in the dressing room the oldest of schools exchange words.

"And yer man across the water Jackson? Eh?"

"They drew boss. At Coventry."

We are five points above the relegation area. Forest are six points ahead of Everton at the top of the First Division and cannot be caught. There is a bitter irony for the black and white half of Nottingham.

"So that's them in the fucking European Cup next season Jackson."

"That so boss."

"Not a bit of it Jackson, not a bit of it. They are top, league champions. It's what this game is about eh? There are results and there are tables. The rest is just fucking opinion, eh Jackson. Aye, fucking opinion."

Jimmy shakes his head but chortles a laugh. This time next week.....

The Newmarket quenches the thirst and is as good a place to spend the win bonus and celebrate. An early morning indulgence of Fairport sat on the balcony. *Who Knows Where the Time Goes* gets the better of *River Man*, the mournful, magnificent voice of Sandy Denny, yet another troubled soul who shuffled of this mortal coil yesterday.

Who's a pretty boy then? The Incredible Hunk, or David Hunt, wooed female and football fans in equal measure. A prolific scorer from the midfield berth.

April 25

IT is a game that will be remembered for a farewell performance from the old wooden stand behind the Meadow Lane end as Sheffield United escape with a 2-1 midweek win. Which is just as well because it's a game I want to forget.

The old girl had been standing obediently, defying her 68 years of age, serving hot teas and cold pies beneath her wooden seats having been there since the ground was built. When performing in the Old Elizabethan League from primary school onwards, our cup finals would be staged at Meadow Lane, usually on the Saturday after a first-team match when County, back then in the 1960s and a pre-Sirrel era, had probably been rolled over 4-0 by Southport or Barrow. Our changing rooms were in the canteen, such as it was, beneath the stand, the smell of liniment, newly-coated thick black paint and half-consumed stale steak and kidney pies laced with Bovril as the ground staff began sweeping up the debris. And then 25 minutes each way on the bone-hard, threadbare pitch that probably reduced a less elderly Peter Thompson (our groundsman was never young surely) to tearing his tonsils out.

And here I was on a similar end-of-season pitch playing like a half-baked clumsy centre-half for Fairham Brook Under-11s and being punished not by Clifton All Whites but Alan Woodward, whose free-kick through our defensive wall evened things up before Keith Edwards smashed one in the top corner from 30 yards.

If the stand was destined to be chopped up for firewood, I felt it should have been me, cremated after a dreadful match, legs like cement on a Bakelite pitch with divots, sneaking away in the hidey-holes like a coward afraid to receive the ball in the channels as one bobble after another takes the ball, with a life of its own, further away from me. Even Pedro is sending out distress signals and search parties trying to find me.

Mike Green, the Torquay manager who wanted to buy me a few months ago, was at the game and spoke to him later.

"Can't think why I wanted to spend five quid on you never mind £5,000 David," he should have said but Mike is too nice a guy to tell the truth.

And Ronnie Fenton was there and no doubt having a laugh. With good cause. He's just won the League title as Cloughie's assistant and he's been watching the shadow man chasing shadows. Should have kept straight on at Torbay to China on a slow boat when I had the chance.

April 29

FOR reasons of his own and beyond my own comprehension, Jimmy retains confidence in me. More sensibly he has also kept faith with a side that for the most part has pulled his club up from the bottom rung to be in touching distance of a magical 38 points and safety. A win will do it for sure, a point might.

And so there is more than a touch of the old guard on parade at the Victoria Ground for the last Saturday of the Second Division season.

Stoke City in eighth are safe but just four points above County's total in a league table that has become tighter than Jack Dunnett's pay rises. Still if I was seeking a performance-related increase, I was fortunate not to have my pay docked on a weekly basis.

Today, though, there is a confidence in the away team dressing room. Sometimes there is the unspoken dread, the suppressed silence and calm of a dressing room in fear or trepidation that even the Billy Brindleys cannot penetrate to lift spirits. But now, 15 minutes before kick-off, it is an unspoken will to get the job done. The April air is Skeggy-bracing, the ground soft underneath, a bit of give unlike the hard-baked lunar-crated surface at Meadow Lane in midweek.

Howard Kendall may lack pace but he could still a pass a ball more elegantly than anyone at this level. Terry Conroy, Viv Busby and Garth Crooks add pace to their guile and Brendan O'Callaghan's height up front.

Deservedly, we are in front. Archie Mann is flying, Carter jinxing on the right, Hunt putting his pretty head in where it hurts. Pedro has smacked the initial volley but Braddy gets the telling touch. 1-0, less than ten minutes to Second Division football. And then Crooks, from a hashed clearance, zooms down on McManus and lashes the equaliser from close range.

A game that we were coasting suddenly is a siege.

"Jesus christ Benjy, get the fucking ball up to the Bomber," Jimmy is frantic on the bench, relaying orders to our hair-intensive substitute to bide for time, for some respite from the pressure with a decent pass to Braddy up front. "Wesley, Wesley, come and get this fucking ball of this boy eh son. Show for him Wesley."

And then: "David, David, get back and tuck in son. Get beyond O'Brien. Jesus Jackson, eh son, it's simple enough eh!" and Jack Wheeler concedes yet another slap on the thigh with his customary good grace, nod of the head and his own exhortations, 'come on David, son' just as motivational as Jimmy's even though deep down you are trying to splurt: "For fuck's sake, I'm trying my best Jack much as I don't want to let you or that bloody foul-mouthed Jock to your left down!"

Injury time drags on, lots of it, far more than seems appropriate. But Stubbs is a rock, like his old self when with Needham. Chapman resolute, Richards swift and crunching in the tackle. Crooks, one last chance, but wide. Well wide. Huge sighs of relief. And then the final whistle.

"You fucking beauties," Sirrel is ecstatic in the dressing room, giving every player a hug and kiss. With Mansfield and Hull City already down, the point is enough to keep us up. "That was a battle, eh Jackson. In the end. But we stood up to it, eh son?"

Colin Slater, on Radio Nottingham no less, has asked for an interview. Seems to think I played reasonably well. Debatable Colin.

Later on, the Newmarket bitter seldom tasted sweeter, even at two in the morning and Greeny on a high, literally, dancing on the tables, which given his neck and bolts was not such a good idea.

May 2

BLACKPOOL, pushing for promotion at Christmas, are submerged in a tangerine nightmare. Despite 37 points, they are down. For us, there is also no escape from the irksome County Cup, the last piece of business before the summer recess for a squad preparing for Spanish beaches or the sun and sand of the builder's yard, earning some cash-in-hand bonuses as opposed to the real winning ones that hibernate for the summer.

In Jimmy's case it would be Gibraltar, Malta or Third Lanark. Or all three. In any case, he had disappeared before the County Cup semi-final at Field Mill which proved not to be an issue. An early exit to Mansfield did the trick leaving them to squeeze in a final against the League champions and League Cup winners at the City Ground in the near or distant future.

"That was without a shadow of a doubt one of the least disciplined performances I have ever seen by a professional footballer," Murphy in charge once again was candid in his post-match analysis. In Mansfield's economical changing room it is difficult to gauge exactly whom he is addressing.

His head hung low and that nervous squint did not help identify the culprit. Neither did that mockney gibberish. The lips were moving but it was impossible to decipher what on earth he was blabbering on about.

"I think he was looking at you McVay," Smithy, a rare first-team appearance, showering with intent to hit the town just as fast as Geoff can navigate the County coach back down the A60 back to civilisation.

"Definitely you Rocky," adds Chapman. "Although that said Smithy, I reckon with that cross-eyed squint of his, he had the pair of you in his sights. Quite fucking right in my opinion."

It was a notable double for me. Last season when flung in for the meaningless match Ronnie had expressed the view that he had seen 'more movement from a milk bottle than I did from you tonight.'

Whatever, whoever Smurf had in mind, walking in the Lakes, drinking in the Lakes, well mostly just drinking was on my mind. Besides I'd taken an instant dislike to the reserve team coach months ago. It saved time.

May 5

FRESH supplies to the beer-thirsty arrive just in time. Another 88 pints of Home Ales seals the top of Eddy's unloaded, unemployed washing machine. There might be amoeba already forming inside the hopeless Hotpoint, a new civilisation emerging not from the sea but Persil suds and skid-marked kecks. In a million years, they might make a better job of it than their marine-based ancestors. But first, they have to find a way past Greeny's flagons of beer. Could their object of worship then be the great Barrel in the Sky known as Home Ales? Or, more worryingly, the great and the good Tony Green, known to non-believers as Frank Einstein of Newmarket? Life's eternal puzzle.

May 6

WILLIE Young Fuck-up 1, Arsenal 0. Fantastic. Wembley belongs to Suffolk.

A midnight kitchen rugby scrum of 10-bearded CAMRA enthusiasts and Ginger Jeff further endear me to the single lady below whose life was serene and normal until about a year or so ago. The police are called. The scrum collapses with the empty Party 7, standing in for rugger's egg, beneath the beer-sodden pile of bodies. *Blowing Free* and *Sea of Joy* see them all off the premises. Somehow flowers aren't going to do it for Mrs Seething in No.29.

May 7/8/9

MIDDAY drive to Keswick, camping out at the Pheasant Inn near Bassenthwaite with Paul. Cultural half an hour in Cockermouth and Wordsworth's house before a free house interrupts for a longer scrutiny.

A walk up Catbells the next day clears the head and a few more pints with Pete and Muriel, friends of the family, in Rossthwaite to follow. And so forth. That is the best thing about the Lakes. When the hills run out, the pubs move in. And vice versa. Perfection.

May 13

SATURDAY back at Clifton Estate. Peggy is leaving to marry an architect George, Pat will be out soon enough with a bloke called Des. I have my doubts but whatever their love lives, it will be the end of a particular era for the house at 19 Listowel. Once the scent and sound of fresh baking and overcrowded but happy families ran through its small rooms and staircase. Outside coal bunkers were machine-gun towers, back gardens and paths the cricket strips and football pitches of the country, from the Oval to Old Trafford. Childhood dreams of a generation of council house dwellers. Today I have a sense of decay, decline and death. In the bedroom mirrors there are only shattered faces, the fight and force gone from Granddad, the raging communist, and Grandma, one of the old-style Northern matriarchs who ran the household and kept it spotless. Even our boxer dog Caesar with a cancer that disfigured his head. I wish it was not so, but I won't be coming back here again.

June 3

WHEN Scotland failed in the last one, I was there, not West Germany but in front of the box on Clifton Estate with Janet Haynes, supporting boyhood hero Denis Law and the tartan hopes of progression in the World Cup finals as well my own progress in the Janet Haynes finals. Both in vain. Still I want them to do well so getting trounced by Peru tonight is not a cause for rejoicing. And for all Masson's faults, I felt for him when he had that penalty saved. Never thought I would think like it but he didn't deserve that. Mind you, Scotland were rank and Peru shit-hot impressive, as they say on Clifton, or so I am told when infrequently visiting from my upmarket city apartment.

June 15

ALAN Groves is dead. He'll never laugh at my surging runs again. Waste of a left-winger and comic. E J Thribb (29 and a half years is far too young).

June 26

THE morning after: Holland once again cheated out of a World Cup final. Not that Peru losing 6-0 to Argentina had anything to do with anything remotely dodgy. And some of the decisions in Buenos Aries. Referee hand-picked by the generals. Enough world football politics. Did I mention Dave Bury's balcony that is twice the size and thrice as impressive as mine. Whereas he once could see Nastase v Connors while quaffing Pimm's on his *al fresco* extension, I am now looking at 20 empty milk bottles, two bedraggled lines of dubious washing, dubious because with the Hotpoint out-of-order and hemmed in by the Home Ales rations, said washing was a hands-on chore with raw Persil in the sink. The glimpse of greenery and the smelting towers of Boots or some factory in the distance interrupts fleetingly between the stacked tins of Party 4s and 7s and bottles of Newkie Brown.

Should the Park Residents' Association be on the prowl, ever vigilant even on a Monday morning, they would demand my notice to quit. The Clumber Court Vigilantes Movement, numbering 28 of 30 members (myself and delightful former pub landlady across the way have refused to join) have already set in motion eviction orders. Alas to no avail as yet.

Hanging out your laundry in public, hand or machine-washed, is not permitted in the rules and regulations as laid down by the Oxford University Chest. Bloody contracts, should have got Jolly Jack to scrutinise before signing. Still if it was good enough for the Siegfried Line, good enough for me. Or was that the Maginot Line?

As for the empties, the milk bottles make for perfect stumps when playing front room cricket with the balcony as a crease. The empty cans are what drive the teams to indulge in the summer pastime. Fortunately No.29 tends to summer with friends on the south coast so play, sometimes floodlit by the single bulb dangling from a frayed wire on the ceiling, is relatively uninterrupted unless the tennis ball beats bat and has to be retrieved from the mangled mess of nettles and thorns that pass for a garden on ground level. Daylight or night time, retrieval of said ball usually ends the game through lack of interest and pub reopening time. Alternatively Plod stops play. Or a broken wicket. Whichever arrives first.

The perm rather than the force went with Dave Smith.

July 10

ANOTHER punishing session in the Turkish steam rooms at the Victoria Baths in Sneinton. It is the footballer's logic that you can sweat out what you have been drinking the night before and with this method of extracting the offending liquid, there is less actual physical pain. Though keeping on the move among the mists of the steam rooms is advisable when little blokes and giant bling come calling on an adjacent bed with towels at half-mast. *Never Let Her Slip Away* pervades the summer night's air walking back through the city centre to the flat. The new fitness regime does not allow a liquid stop at any of the public houses. Besides, it's Monday, nobody is out and the students are on holiday.

July 28

TRYING hard to get motivated for the new season. Futile. It should not be this way but every aching bone in my body after the usual arduous pre-season stint up Colwick Woods and Wilford Tip beg to differ.

Indeed they were standard, fixed points on the summer compass, almost old friends in fact. But Meadow Lane was a moving, shifting landscape now.

The wooden stand was not the only departure from the landscape. Braddy's vital goal at Stoke a few months earlier turned out to be his last one for Notts before moving to Stockport County. Jeff Blockley, who has England caps on his CV and eclipses Birchenall in the dropping-a-name game, has signed on.

Put it one way, he frequently held audiences spellbound listing his top 100 players, in reverse order, but seldom got beyond number 90 by which time, Bobby Moore, Malcolm Macdonald, Gerd Muller and Kevin Keegan had been mentioned in dispatches without selection just to whet the appetite.

He had groomed his black hair in the Keegan bubble but with a matching moustache, the image of Blockers in a leather jacket and peaked cap in a New York dungeon presented itself far too often for my liking.

July 31

MANSFIELD in summer. An Anglo-Scottish Cup tie to be played in north Nottinghamshire. Made perfect sense.

Still there were significant additions from our previous encounter as well as Blockley. Iain McCulloch is a winger Sirrel has plucked from Kilmarnock. His pace was as intimidating as his physical aggression but we feared that if he learnt to flap his ears in tandem with his legs during one his forward forages and, with the wind in the right direction, then somewhere near the County Road corner flag he might achieve lift off and retain a respectable cruising altitude until well past Melton Mowbray. In comparison, Ricky Green was very much more grounded, talking in a bumpkin drawl, languid in movement with a knack of scoring goals in the lower leagues. Signed from Chesterfield as a target man, his remit is to replace Bradd. It may be a tough winter for the slow-talking striker.

Another uninspired stroll around Field Mill and subbed. Finishing on survival and such a high last time at Stoke's Victoria Ground, just can't seem to get my mind on the season ahead.

August 1

COLIN King, our reserve goalkeeper with a John Travolta take on fashion and a Demis Roussos take on diet, is unimpressed as the Cortina ricochets off parked cars on High Pavement, dodgems in front of the old court house. "Christ Rocky, you nearly hit that one." Chapman is in the front seat awaiting arrival at a late night drinking establishment.

Two hours earlier we had been beaten by Leicester City in the Bass Charity Vase final at Burton Albion's ground. Jimmy had not been impressed with my contribution at Field Mill last night. "Aye, get your sharpness and fitness with a game tonight eh son." Translated, get your arse in gear and act together you lazy sod if you want to play in my first-team this season.

I could have argued that perhaps it was a gyspy curse laid on me by bleach-boy that turned my legs to jelly and my attitude to apathetic at Field Mill but I got the feeling Jimmy would not have been amused. Still, Field Mill and me don't seem to have got on very well over the years.

The Bass Vase, football's most expensive trophy, is strictly second XI stuff. The winners get a nice trophy and a nice medal apiece. The losers got a bottle of whisky. Each. With three Johnny Walkers drained on the back seat of the coach on the short trip back to Meadow Lane, heads were obliged to roll, particularly in the back of the Cortina. Nodding dogs Smithy and King are anxious. Chapman doesn't care. His contract is up and we all know he has a transfer sorted for the new season. So just the one for the road … or ditch.

It will end in tears and the Arriba. For Chapman, beaming on all the pre-season team photographs last week, it's laughter all the way to the bank with a move and tidy signing-on fee to Shrewsbury which he says will be sorted this week.

August 19

NEW season, same old problems. A 5-2 defeat at West Ham United. 4-0 down after 20 minutes, Blockers put one though his own net on his league debut for us, hassled by Trevor Brooking, who moved from top 20 material to lower 40s in our perm-headed central defender's all-time top 100 list.

August 23

"SMITHY, you were always a dirty little sod," the oft repeated truism uttered by Don Masson who was enjoying a late night bottle of Champagne in the Arriba.

In fact, no-one was quite sure if it was French bubbly that was being drunk by his retinue despite a label that indicated its Gallic provenance.

Masson the Merciless was now Masson the Mellowness, holding court in the middle bar with several dispensable reserve team players, though none were more instantly disposable than Smithy and myself.

"But I thought Derby were playing tonight," Smithy quizzes.

"Injured son. But watch this space. Another bottle of … whatever this is and some orange juice to take the taste away please!"

August 28

A WEEK later and dutifully watching all spaces, Flash Carter is flushed out of Meadow Lane to Derby while Masson returns in the opposite direction from the Baseball Ground.

Almost four years since he departed to a rapturous dressing room, Masson arrives to an altered squad and like his mentor Sirrel, he too appears changed, championed for his midfield skills and role as Scotland captain but perhaps chastened by that missed penalty against Peru which did little to quell mutiny in the ranks of Ally's expectant Army.

At any rate, he is welcomed back warmly by all and sundry, not least Sirrel whose arms are wider open than most now that he is reunited with his 'jewel in the crown'.

The Bolton left-back and the expectant Main Stand crowd have no idea which way Flash Carter is going to turn or when he will release the ball. The same applied to his team-mates in the middle. Normally clinical from 12-yards, he departed in typically unpredictable fashion by fluffing a penalty in his final game against Millwall.

September 8

MY only meaningful contribution to the weekend task of collecting Division Two points is being part of the Friday seven-a-side squad that is the first-team's prelude to a Saturday league fixture.

Practice matches had declined, only fractionally, under the new Sirrel, and the seven-a-sides seemed to be an initiative influenced by Masson. The 'wee fellow' speaks and Sirrel listens. Alternative lines of communication are futile.

Gone are the bruising encounters on the ash and gravel car park that often ended in Friday fisticuffs under the regime of Mick Jones when he was Ronnie's No.2, a case of poacher turned gamekeeper when he returned to County. Jonah had a habit of dangling lucrative carrots to the younger pros before North Midlands League games, how they might be driving around in a posh car, a Beamer or Merc, if they pulled their finger out and made a name for themselves, a tactic apparently in vogue and working the oracle over at Clough's City Ground. Whatever Jonah's thinking, given some of the younger pros from Derby and their connections in the motor trade, they probably could have been swanning about in an S Class anyway, fully resprayed and renumbered to order.

Mick had been a leader of the social pack and a solid, reliable defender to have on your side with County's two great promotion teams of the early 1970s. Still one of his first duties as great white coach was to 'nick' Smithy and myself for a late session in Mr Miller's two whole days before a reserve game. The fine was immaterial. The irony not so. Without doubt you need skin as thick as rhino hide allied with chameleon-like deception and loyalty to take the quantum leap to the other side of the white line and the dugout mentality. It's just not appreciated by those who knew you before you gained a stripe on the arm and a foot on the greasy pole of management. Probably why those players are the first ones moved on to pastures new.

Now Masson was more or less second in command, those fractious Fridays were replaced by a more civilised option on grass at Wilford Tip.

However, some traditions have not been abandoned entirely. O'Brien still challenges Jimmy in bending the best free-kick over or around the mobile 'wooden wall' on wheels, cardboard cut-outs with head-shaped defences along the top of the castle.

And the Yellow Bib remains the equivalent of the classroom Dunce's Cap, to be worn in the corner of the dressing room for several minutes as a shameful penance for the worst performance on Friday morning. A new venture is a chocolate bar for the best player.

Masson directs traffic as Jack Wheeler prepares to referee the contest. "Jack, you count the nutmegs. The player who gets the most against him gets the bib. The player who scores the most nutmegs gets the chocolate. Simple."

Jack has the Sirrel whistle in his mouth on peep-peep stand-by.

"One thing though Jack. If anyone megs Ricky, it doesn't count."

Laughter all around. Even Green sees the funny side. New Masson certainly is much better than the previous incarnation but when it comes to a barb or quip, some old habits were proving harder to kick than others.

September 10

FREE bar at the Delisle Arms. The Barney Wilds has landed four days ago, brother to Natalie. His dad John reckons he'll play for Forest one day. Or County. Or Leicester. His mum wants to sleep. Uncle David commences the toasts to his nephew and niece and a father who knows his beer far better than his football. The best kind of landlord.

September 14

A PRACTICE match on the pitch, much to Peter's dismay. After a win at Leicester Ricky keeps his place in the first-team and scores two as the reserves are routed 6-1. Big Killer is not at his best, proof provided after one of Jimmy's classic post-whistle rebukes.

In the morning sunshine, he is perched on one of the crush barriers on the terraces of the deserted County Road stand, serenely surveying the first XI taking apart the remainder of us when the blue touch paper is ignited.

Having sounded the alarm, a fierce, piercing blast of his trusted whistle, he skips over the advertising hoardings and is marching with more than intent towards our penalty area where Kilcline has just been brushed aside, allowing Ricky to score his second of the match in facile manner. The big smile on Killer's face is not helping his case or improving Jimmy's demeanour.

"Ey son, ey, aye you big boy, have I done something to fucking offend you son?"

It is normally at this juncture that brave men run for cover and cowards run for the hills. An explosion is imminent and it is not going to end well for anybody in the vicinity.

"No boss. Why?" responds Killer, the teenager in him still believing he can engage his master in meaningful banter.

"Why son? Because you are fucking offending me, eh? What the fucking hell is that son? A tackle?"

"I was trying not to foul him boss, inside the area." Ah, the rashness of youth. Killer has not quite grasped that you don't answer back, remain rigid with chin up and take the bollocking like a man.

"Och, you didnae want to foul him in the penalty area?" the tone is mocking now. "Aye, well let him past son, no trouble eh. Who do you think you are son? Beckenbauer, eh? Rudi Krol eh? Not a bit of it! Jackson! Give me that ball, now you run at me Killer son."

Jack rolls the ball to Kilcline's feet and he is forced to try and get past Jimmy in the 18-yard box knowing full well that he is destined for a whack on the shins and a rapid fall to the ground.

"Listen son, you take no prisoners, eh? Understand. Look at the size of yez? Yez never, ever let anyone that side of you son. Jesus christ, Jackson, look at the size of this boy and he's showing people the ball and letting them muscle him off the fucking thing. Up, up, now let's see some fucking tackling from you boys in the yellow bibs."

Us boys in the yellow bibs being the reserves have seen it all before, usually the target of the gaffer's practical lesson, as have most of the first-team, except the 'wee fellow' of course who can't resist a wry smile as Jimmy jogs back to his vantage point in the County Road stand. "Let's play Jackson!" he urges and we're mostly having a laugh now in the yellow bibs. We have been spared. Our turn next week. Unless Killer fails to raise his game.

September 16

MASSON'S home debut on his return and a winning goal late on. Obviously drinks in the Centenary Club prevented a first-hand viewing but a gust of wind apparently blew in a corner three minutes from time. The anointed one is well and truly restored to his exalted place.

September 17

NOBODY back at Clifton now. Pat has moved out to a maisonette up Donkey Hill in St Ann's, another region like the Meadows that is part of the council's visionary slum clearance programme. This is relatively new and clean, views all over the city centre. On a clear day you can see the Victoria Centre flats like the carbuncle it is and the remainder of St Ann's stretching up the Well's Road, ripe for more demolition or cheap student accommodation. The Beacon pub is virtually parked outside the block of maisonettes so a Sunday pint is in order. It seems so sanitised, like much of the new-build homes hastily erected in this part of the old St Ann's. Incongruous, displaced people. Maybe just me. Pat seems happy enough. Maybe she is.

September 21

ALTHOUGH they get a bad press in general, I tend to get on with students. The attraction must be because they are young, have an abundance of spare time and are inclined to social habits and drinking that could be best described as excessive. There are six of them living in a Victorian wreck of a house at the bottom end of the Park in Hope Drive, two of them girls, and the beauty in numbers means that if one of them is actually studying (highly unlikely) there are five other options available for duty in the Newmarket. Frankenstein prefers the girls to make an appearance but when the screws loosen in his neck, they are perfectly safe to drink real ale while avoiding Ginger Jeff's scalp.

September 25

THERE is a message in the front office for me. "Mike Green, from Torquay, would like you call him on this number David," secretary Dennis Marshall announces. I hadn't seen him since last season when I hardly covered myself in glory against Sheffield United. Surely on that evidence he didn't want me back at Plainmoor? With no phone at the flat, the nearest phone box from the ground is on Iremonger Road. After a brief pause, the club receptionist puts me through. A few pleasantries then: "What can you tell me about Dave Smith?"

Plenty, I thought, but not much you would want to know.

"Why, how do you mean?"

"I'm thinking of signing him on."

Long pause, to get over my disappointment that he wasn't coming in for me.

"You still there David?"

"Yes Mike. What do you want to know?"

"Well, what sort of a lad is he? Good for the dressing room?"

Most players have had this sort of interrogation from a manager who wants to put a few gentle feelers out for a player he fancies signing. The man asking the questions wants to get an inside track on the player without consulting his manager. The player answering is trying to balance fact and fiction, not lie to his inquisitor but above all make sure his teammate gets the best possible CV.

"Brilliant for dressing room morale Mike (when we see him exiled in his piles bath, it gives us all a lift)."

"Is his reliable David?"

"Totally consistent Mike (consistently playing the clown)."

"What about his character?"

"Oh a real character Mike (always just one slap or punch away from a good hammering having concealed the underpants or socks of nearly every senior pro after training during his apprenticeship days)."

"But can he play?"

"Oh yes he can play right enough (and he could)."

With a sense of having done right by Smithy but wishing sincerely that one day all this wouldn't rebound on me I said cheerio to one of the game's truly good guys hoping that it wasn't the last goodbye.

October 1

MRS Beyond Seething and Driven to Distraction at No.29 vented her spleen this morning. "You must have been dragged up in the most uncouth manner. You can tell you've come from the council estate," she mused with an uncanny truth, slamming my door in my face at around 4am. Roman orgies certainly had less bodies but probably more motion and definitely more women and horses than the scene upstairs. The Hope Drive hippies have met CAMRA's hardcore and there isn't a beardless chin in the house. It's time to stop this nonsense. It's time Greeny stopped sending those barrels of beer as well.

October 10

AT the Odeon, alone, for *Annie Hall*. Why? Diane Keaton. Nothing else really came close.

October 21

I HAVE fond memories of Kenilworth Road, holding Luton to 1-1 draw here years ago with Barry Butlin in his pomp. That was a time when Jimmy trusted me to play centre-half if Stubbs or Needham were injured. Today as sub, and 2-0 down at half-time, he unleashes me in the unseasonal winter sun.

Even for Jimmy he is scathing of the performance during the tea interval, nobody is spared his wrath and Hunty is hauled off leaving me and Stubbsy at the back with Benjy pushed into midfield.

"See what you can do David, to keep this defence tight with Brian, eh?"

No sooner said than done boss. It's 3-0 three minutes later and double that by the end, that little bastard Brian Stein sneaking one in a minute from time when I assumed I had it covered. 6-0. Mission accomplished.

October 27

FOR some reason, Jimmy has foisted the blame for that Luton drubbing on Pedro. Unfit, unprofessional, unwilling to work, Pedro is line for the Idi Amin award of most unloved tyrant of the decade. Most of us think it is unfair but then the gaffer has a different agenda. As usual he was back late from his Spanish siesta at the village where he was raised in northern Spain, a family relative mysteriously passes away just as he was about to return for pre-season training. Jimmy usually lets it go but now Pedro's name is not on the team sheet for the game with Cambridge tomorrow. He's put me at No.2 in his place. The poisoned chalice.

October 28

"AYE son, yerve got the opposition and the crowd against you today David."

Thanks for the words of encouragement boss. Pedro is such a crowd favourite and a local Meadows lad, you can almost hear the groans when I get my first touch. At least I feel comfortable at the back again. McCulloch scores his first goal at Meadow Lane. 1-1. The County team get a draw with Cambridge; a home defeat for the No.2 with some of the fans.

November 4

PEDRO'S punishment in exile continues though who is suffering the most is a matter of debate. Wrexham's Racecourse Ground is grey, drab and uninviting unlike the team who are full of livewires. It was a case of should I? shouldn't I? but I knew the instant I tried to nick the ball off Graham Whittle it was the wrong move while the referee made the right decision, the penalty being converted by Mickey Thomas. 2-1 became three and my sojourn at right-back is all but over.

November 11

PEACE has broken out between Jimmy and Pedro, who is restored to right-back. A not too unfamiliar seat on the bench is my reward for keeping the full-back berth warm for its rightful owner's return, responding with the sort of mighty display that his penance warranted. Swift into the tackle, incisive on the overlap and composed on the ball, West Ham don't get a look-in. Devonshire, Holland, county or country, they're all the same, none shall pass Pedro, or Archie Mann and Stubbsy at the heart of defence for that matter. Mind you, Jimmy has deployed Benjy as an extra defender and is defending deep, allowing the visitors to attack but denying them in the last third. Having conceded five at Upton Park on the first day of the season and six at Luton Jimmy is taking no chances. He's used this ploy before and it works again.

A lesson in tactics and man-management though a scare late on when he asks me to warm up. Well not directly. He uses Jack Wheeler, sitting betwixt the two of us as a conduit. More an echo chamber. Jimmy tells Jack to tell me to warm up and Jack, having duly told me, then turns to tell Jimmy that I have been informed of my impending departure from bench to pitch and will be warming up on the running track. However on this occasion, I have lost my shinpads among Jack's liniments and oils and there is a delay in attracting the referee's attention as a David Cross header is saved majestically by Eric Mac.

"Get that fucking boy on Jackson, pads or no fucking pads," Jimmy is fulminating in the dugout, one eye on the tense finale as the clarets forge forward yet again, bellowing to Pedro to get the ball upfield, and one eye on Jack, who tells me to pull my socks up, get the tie-ups sorted and myself on the pitch. Fuck! If they score now Jimmy will either spontaneously combust or strangle me with my tie-ups. Or strangle Jack to show him how it's done then tell him to strangle me.

Mercifully just as I am contemplating my demise by slow strangulation at the hands of Jack or Jimmy, or both, and a dirty old piece of rewashed nylon tie-up, Jack escorts me to the halfway line as the full-time whistle blows. Jimmy is beside himself, euphoric with the two points and clean sheet, raging that I had not managed to earn my win bonus by virtue of a 20-second trot on the pitch. Apart from my undeserved £80, the Smurf leaves for Lincoln City. Maybe good things come in twos.

NOVEMBER 11 1978:
Photo call before the home win over West Ham United. But where are the shin pads for the man in slightly bulging blue tracksuit standing next to the chap in the tasteful yellow ensemble? For those watching in black and white, they are back row, far left.

November 18

WITH shinpads firmly clasped by both hands, I am No.12 at Ewood Park and a novel experience in the sodden Blackburn air. McVay replacing Masson. One minute remaining. It is 3-3 when Hunty lashes one into the top corner. Didn't have the time or the legs to catch his celebration.

November 29

VIV makes his England debut tonight, the first black lad to play for the full national side. Never mind the colour, he's got to be the first Clifton lad to represent his country at this level. Oppressed of the world sure to rejoice at the historic double.

December 9

ALL good things must come to an end.

"The bastards have finally lost a game," Pete Quilty, poised with whisky chaser in the Centenary Club was in a mood to rejoice. Not so much that we had just given league leaders Crystal Palace a 'right good hiding', as he put it, in a 0-0 draw but that Nottingham Forest had lost at Liverpool 2-0.

"Yep but it has taken 42 games and just over a year for it to happen," someone pointed out.

"No the bubble has burst m'duck, definitely burst."

It's been a bloody slow puncture then Pete.

December 25

CHRISTMAS drinks in the Loggerheads. Burnt bird in the oven, too late to save it. Save it from what? Too late for the poor sod now, torched beyond recognition. Alone in the flat. Hankering for a white Christmas, a Morecambe and Wise Christmas. A proper family Christmas. With the trimmings but without the christ bit. In truth, I quite like it like this. Today: sweet and sour extremely crispy turkey. Tomorrow: Oldham.

December 26

JIMMY insists on taking a squad of 16 players for most games, a tactic started by Ronnie and probably continued to keep four of his senior players off the streets and out of the bars back in Nottingham. Makes sense. Still it's only the first-named 12 who get the bonus so the only incentive for the remainder is to compile the definitive good beer guide to the players' bars and general hospitality around Football League grounds. From Craven Cottage to Roker Park, there have been three or four stars (out of five) but nothing compares to the obliging entertainment at Boundary Park where we are invited into the directors' suite to see the second half on tap, unquenchable thirst nurtured by an unbroken supply of lager at the front of the glass boxes which open out into the freezing Boxing Day air in one of Manchester's less salubrious satellite towns.

It is hard, gruelling work but somehow Ricky and myself are able to keep a focus through the frost and chilled lager when Blockley, on as sub, levels for 3-3. Another unbeaten game, another payless day as the 15th travelling man. O'Brien, possibly in Blockley's top 100 Irish full-backs list but not in my top 100 Irish drinkers list (admittedly tough competition) is honking up in the back seat of the coach. Hooks is overflowing into a bottle of brimming-over urine. Jimmy is ignoring it all at the front. A point is a good return and after all it is the festive season. Better still we are on the road leading out and far away from Oldham.

December 30

THE body-sprayers convention Christmas outing was a little late in coming, a little light on attendance and a little short on transport. But I did not mind. It was a pleasure to drive Dream-on Dixie and Big Al to the scene of County's great escape in the Potteries last season even if Pokey Stokey just didn't seem an appropriate venue to extend the festive spirit.

The landscape was seasonal, though. A few miles beyond the Salt Box cafe on the A50, the snow begins to fall.

Dixie was regaling a story of sexual bondage, something to do with his towing ropes, a barmaid in Arnold and the nozzle on his spray gun but he lost me when he started waxing lyrical about the suction power of his car vacuum cleaner.

"Listen this snow is getting worse. Where is this fucking ground?"

"You should know David."

"Played there not bloody driven there Alan. That's what Geoff does when he drives the coach."

"Perhaps he should play and you drive in future."

"Very good Dixie. Is it left here?"

"Yeh then just park where you can."

Vinter had left tickets for our little excursion which continued inside the snow-stricken Victoria Ground but the party arrived too late to see Sammy Irvine score inside two minutes for the home team.

"It was Pedro's fault," shouts Dixie once seated and gradually freezing in the main stand. "No definitely Benjy's," replies Big Al.

"No it was definitely me." Was it really just a few short months ago in the April spring sunshine that I was part of a magical moment, feeling so much involved in the club and its salvation? The hugs and embraces were heartfelt on that day but it seems so distant now, not a part of the first-team plans at all, 18th man at worst, 12th man at best. Smithy and Lloyd Richards are not even that far up the ladder but I already know how that feels and once more I was heading down that path again. Part and parcel of the modern game son, as Brindley always told me. 'One day you're flavour of the month, next you're flavour of dog pooh'. Or something like that. Currently, sat shivering in the well-ventilated stadium, I felt someone somewhere was wiping me off the bottom of their newly polished shoes like mutt excrement.

McCulloch's dash, Masson's guile, Benjamin's pace all to no avail in the blinding snow that was sweeping in from the west and settling predominantly on the pitch and my nose. Even the magnificent Matthews, the Wizard of the Dribble, may have found his wing craft in disarray on his home turf in his native Potteries

"Time to go," Dixie calls after O'Callaghan slotted in a second ten minutes from time.

Mercifully the white Cortina has not been stolen on this occasion, camouflaged in the snow that has now reached Stalingrad siege levels.

I think all the County fans have had the same bloody idea as what appeared a wagon train of Notts supporters trailed cautiously along the A50.

"Get out and push," I told Dixie and Big Al after the Cortina stalled on a gradient on a B-road diversion suggested by the works outing committee. "It's your fucking car and your fucking route. And I'm going to be late for my own party."

"But you're younger, stronger and fatter, you get out," protested Dixie. The logic was incontestable.

"This is the last bleeding car I buy from you pair."

Three hours later, the 1978 festive fun was over. Officially.

"See you later," I suggested dropping the pair off in a snow-laden city centre.

"Nobody is going to come out in this tonight. Not in the Park with all those hills. Taxis won't touch it." Dixie the optimist.

"Suppose you'll be tied up this evening."

"I fucking hope so."

By ten o'clock, music on, wine, spirits, a few crisps, yet another barrel of Green's grog from the Newmarket and all was ready.

Invitations had been sent verbally to the Loggerheads, Newmarket, Notts County, some old school mates, some geeky, some not so, and the Hope Drive hippies.

Did anyone turn up? Not a soul.

12.15am. Bottle of Bowmore malt opened, volume upped on Nick Drake. Since time had not told him or me very much lately, *River Man* seemed apt. Just to cheer myself up.

December 31

POSITIVE thinking is the order of the last day of 1978. After waking up on the floor late in the afternoon, shaved and walked through the Park and its frosting of freshly-fallen crisp snow.

Even on Sunday the Salutation and other city centre pubs had a special licence to serve from five until midnight and beyond if necessary.

Smithy conveys the good news having rung him from the Sal's phone box next to the gent's toilets. The home game against Sheffield United tomorrow has been called off. Meadow Lane is icebound.

Several celebratory Stella Artois dull the senses. Just as well with the Calverton Chapter of the Hell's Angels in residence and full sway upstairs.

A meeting of minds ensues. A bloke with tattoos on his tongue; a girl resembling Donna, sweet and sour sausages Donna, and another with designs on biting my neck rather than my sausages, which was perhaps for the best, for her sake at any rate.

Smithy and Pedro ride in to my neck's rescue, it feeling like it's done ten rounds with George Foreman and 90 minutes with Billy Bremner's studs. The town is dusted in snow, the Market Square almost idyllically festive. The gruesome twosome head for the midnight bells at Scamps. I sneak off to the flat. From Ronnie to Jimmy, through Torquay and other ports of call. Know my time is coming to an end at Meadow Lane. Look forward not back, they say. But can't help dwelling in the past, for the present. Nick Drake, Yes and Argus. Fucking hell, it's a time warp of solitary despondency and regressive despair. And would you have it any other way McVay? Not on this December 31.

1979

January 5

THE FA Cup begins this weekend though the tie with Reading has already been called off. The pitch has a blanket topping of packed snow. Can't help but hark back to last season's run that ended at Millwall. Not that I have a shout of playing in the third round, just confirmation of my sinking status. Are policeman getting younger? Or am I getting more bitter by the day? Even the apprentices are getting cockier. Once a few bob would have had them cleaning your boots with extra polish and relish and on time, now the little bastards are holding out for a £1 and aren't too happy at that either. The peasants' revolt? Wat Tyler? And we all know how he ended up. Then images of a Peterloo-style massacre in Lytham St Annes as a band of rebellious brother apprentices from around the country, congregating outside the Football League HQ, chanting slogans with unpolished boots and placards daubed in dubbin to hand as Jimmy launches a vicious attack of managers and senior pros, leading the cavalry before lancing a few novices from Preston to Portsmouth to quell the revolution. Heads roll, up above Alan Hardaker nods approvingly from his office window.

Jack, bereft of his ukulele and George Formby sing-a-longs, another long-observed ritual that has disappeared from the afternoon dressing room, bemoans the lack of standards.

"Don't know they are born this lot, David. We had to paint the stands, sweep the terraces and clear the snow off the pitch, and all after training which usually ended with a 10-mile road run."

With most people, you'd put that down as exaggeration as reviewed through ruddy-tinged spectacles but with Jack you are fairly sure it's about right. As someone who dodged the apprenticeship route, who am I to complain? Not that it stops me anyway.

Underrated in his early days at Meadow Lane, badly over-exposed latterly in a photogenic faux pas. Apart from his shirt, things were seldom black and white for Paul Hooks.

January 15

ANOTHER idle weekend after the game against Leicester was called off. Birchenall is not pleased, having wanted to prove a point to his former club. He seeks solace in his hair. Seldom are the blond locks less than pristinely shampooed and he even deigns to apply a variety of herbal smellies to his scalp in the communal bath water relatively safe in the knowledge that the sport of turd-surfing has been banned at Meadow Lane. And that is only the beginning.

Like watching an artist in action at his canvas, he first dries the offending hair with one of the wafer-thin numbered blue rags that pass for towels before reaching for his trusty hairdryer.

It is a turbo-charged, fuel-injected model that he totes around the country, his first concern on away trips to locate a plug socket that is within flex-distance of mirror, preferably positioned at a height to correspond to his hirsute requirements. Namely, to blow dry and style the hair in such a manner that it is spread evenly around his head, with just a hint of distress as if to suggest that no effort whatsoever has been expended to create the final look and appearance. At most grounds there is hardly sufficient room in the mirror for Birchenall, his hair dryer, brush, comb and frantically waving arms like a whirling dervish or Mr Teasy-Weasy on speed, hogging the reflection. When the travelling hairdryer makes its daily appearance at Meadow Lane, Birchenall reveals it with the panache of a gunslinger, Doc Holliday at the OK

Corral. Like lightning, easily the fastest draw in the East Midlands.

Only Benjy, with a comb that resembles a demented tuning fork, puts up any sort of defiance in the battle for mirror supremacy. More often a losing one, resigning himself to pluck away at his Afro until it expands to fill the rear view mirror and two front seats of his Ford Cortina. For the rest of us, it's a case of the straggly, natural wet look. There is no other choice.

January 20

SUB at Orient. Managed a brief appearance in awful 3-0 defeat, a whippet called John Chiedozie scores the third. If he'd dropped a gear it might have made the struggle fairer. When did win monies become so frigging hard to come by? And no chance of a Cup bonus next week either after this Brisbane Road non-performance. Played myself out of the fourth round tie at Highbury with consummate ease.

January 27

I AM marvelling at the marble halls and players' room free tuck and booze at Highbury as 17th man in another 16-man squad that travelled to North London for the Cup tie. Definitely five star with merit in the Good Players' Bar Guide.

We are duly dumped out on a partially frozen surface against a distinctly average Arsenal. Willie Young and Brian Talbot score two late goals to secure the home team's safe passage. It could have been Willie Wonka and a Hillman Talbot for all I knew, busy consuming the splendid hospitality and Holsten Pils offered by the decidedly classy VIP suite.

The superior lager sent my mind drifting, nothing unusual except at 4.15 on a Saturday afternoon it was rudely premature.

So severe was my afternoon euphoria that I began to think nice thoughts about Ronnie. Well he was a County pioneer of sorts, taking the squad beyond the shores of Gibraltar to Kenya two summers ago, onwards to the brothels of Nairobi and the white sands of Mombasa and the Indian Ocean.

Such tranquillity and so nearly a perfect holiday with an unhappy ending after Smithy's beach chalet room, which he shared with John Sims, was looted by local tribesmen from the surrounding bush and woods.

"If you had been awake in your room, they would have cut your throat without thinking David," our Kenyan guide Noah told him the following morning.

Instead Smithy and Sims were comatose, totally out of it on booze. Reprieved by liquor then, and saved by lust from a fatal poleaxing in the back seat of the Ford Corsair over a year ago. Smithy's luck surely could not hold.

Nurse, the pils please.

And the little git was at the booze again in Magaluf two years ago, another first for us as Ronnie jetted off his first-teamers for five days in the January sun to restore hopes in what had become a flagging Second Division promotion push.

Of course I only made the trip because of injuries and Steve Carter and Arthur Mann's fear of flying. Perhaps Probert suffered aerophobia also which would explain his bottle of Luton Airport duty free whisky emptied before touchdown in Palma. It was a booze-fest from start to finish, a vodka-inspired Pedro chatting up two girls in perfect Spanish on the shuttle coach to the hotel to be jilted on arrival by two senoritas from Macclesfield.

The other vacancy on the flight was filled by Gordon Mair, our fragile Scottish apprentice who made Twiggy appear as Mama Cass and whom I had forgiven for his earlier indiscretions and liberties taken with my right shin. The squad, and Smithy in particular, was able to instruct him in the ways of drinking Spanish lager by the litre glass by which time he had also cottoned on to the knack of walking home on the roofs of parked cars as if he were a veteran at the urban sport whose origins may emanate from Liverpool or Clifton Estate.

I was just about to reminisce on day two of the Magaluf jaunt when Ronnie threatened to send the entire drunken squad home when I heard footsteps and the sound of people approaching the VIP lounge.

Shit, final whistle. Drain the last half pint of pils.

"Bad luck lads, could have been worse, could have been 2-0," I announced in the away team dressing having anaesthetised several security stewards and two Arsenal apprentices with beer fumes in the players' tunnel.

"It was 2-0 McVay. Had a good afternoon socialising have we?" Vinter dripping with sarcasm.

"Average, thankyou Michael," I replied as coolly as my flushed face would allow.

February 9

WHATEVER the outcome of the game, there would have been no doubt that it was a simple black and white affair. In the event, the two striped Magpies of the Second Division, Notts County and Newcastle United, were prevented from a possible colour clash at St James' Park as snow in the North East caused the game to be called off a day before it was scheduled to go ahead.

For me and the rest of the reserves fodder, it meant another trip to Hyson Green for a morning session.

"Aye David, here's the keys to the minibus son. Take these young men for an hour, a quick chuke-up and some basic skills, eh. Breenge a few balls at the young goalkeeper. I'll leave it up to you son."

Christ, maybe Dixie and Big Al had got it right after all, perhaps the gaffer is grooming me to take over as bus driver from Geoff. Or maybe he thinks that's where my best future lies. I mean Alex Gibson, our former centre-half and a smashing bloke, had donned a black tie and peak cap and was chauffeur to Jolly Jack and his Rolls Royce. Maybe a vacancy was arising? Would have to self-destruct off Trent Bridge with the chairman securely strapped in the back seat. Could there be a more selfless sacrifice to the cause?

Still, from leading the reserves at Scunthorpe for 90 minutes to a minibus driver and coach at Hyson Green for an hour was crab-like progress surely. Not quite demotion. Not yet.

It was a lively session, some basic skills, not so basic skills and a seven-a-side with the apprentices. I noted the deftness of young Mair's touch and footwork patently gleaned from his nifty car roof tops work in Magaluf, a source of immense pride to me.

Similarly Kilcline's touch had improved a little though I knew his physical tackling and heading strength had progressed beyond all reasonable expectations in the last year.

I knew that because while I was being put out to pasture for a summer transfer away from Meadow Lane, I grazed at Bootham Crescent, Boothferry Park, The Shay and the rest of the North Midlands reserve league circuit in relative serenity.

That consisted of dropping deep in what the television pundits were calling the sweeper's role while Killer, all 16-stone muscle and 17-years of age, attacked the ball, player and any other obstacle in his way in what most pundits would call a character-building role. I preferred the Kamikaze Killer position.

Subsequently, while I escaped serious facial injury, tidied up the scant loose ball or players that escaped Kilcline's attention, my centre-half partner's game developed markedly along with several scars, bruises and the odd slightly mashed facial bone.

It was perfect harmony and upon returning to the Arriba, I was able to further teach Killer the art of midnight drinking, a subject that the eager pupil was keen to study and perfect. Grade A student in the making, I was convinced.

With almost avuncular pride I was looking over these young charges with a purring warmth inside. It was good to put something positive back into the game.

Sirrel was delighted when we returned intact but more relieved that the Ford Transit was back in one piece as well. It had cost the club £2,000.

"David, I know you dinna have to son, but the A team have a game at Grove Farm in the morning. It's against the Forest and I always like to put up a good show if possible, eh. Could you help them out eh, take charge, son. They are just a bunch of wee babbies. Would you do that for me son?"

"Of course boss."

"Well done David. Aye and remember you are representing the football club eh son."

"Of course boss."

I represented Notts County in style that night. Normally with the first-team game called off, there would have been an uncanny telepathy urging all players to meet in the Flying Horse at 7pm. Either that or the equivalent of the Bat Signal in the sky, obviously in this case a flying magpie sent from Brindley's Ruddington residence alerting all fit and able players to rendezvous at the Market Square hostelry.

But with the likes of Brindley, Bradd and Probert gone, the nucleus of the team's solidly reliable drinking unit had disappeared. Blockley, O'Brien, McCulloch were simply not up to the task.

However, the Newmarket always offered succour as long as old money and a sixpenny piece was about a person so

I settled for several hours trying to spot Ginger Jeff's scalp lumps discussing the merits of real ale, a stroll to the Old Corner Pin and the Dog and Partridge, Dog and Puff as it was fondly known for its clientele, with a final flurry in the Peach Tree.

With Jimmy's stirring words ringing in my ears, I had planned a route designed to avoid Bottle Lane and a trip to the Arriba and thus the risk of carnal temptations, using George Best as my inspiration. I calculated 10 pints of Home bitter, a takeaway curry and home before midnight was a sufficiently professional attitude for an A team fixture, usually sides brimming with schoolboys on trial or apprentices or soon-to-be discarded old pros.

Through a fog, I remember catching the late night news on television and hearing that Brian Clough had signed Trevor Francis from Birmingham City for £1million before collapsing in a heap on the settee with the pungent aroma of chicken madras wafting me into a deep sleep.

February 10

AWAKE, still dark but after a couple of hours in a comfy bed, it's time to shift. The match kicks off at 10.45am. It is 9.35.

The brushing of teeth trumps underarm cleanliness as does chiselling out the dry madras from a stubbly chin. Trumping of course then leads to the repetitive toilet visits that are the unavoidable aftermath of a Bengal Tiger gastronomic experience.

By 10 I am done. Locate boots and pads which I had brought from the ground the day before and out of the flat.

The venue is a 15-minute drive if the Cortina behaves itself, driving south out of town towards the Trent. It is a cold, dismal, drizzly and stodgy Saturday morning. Could it get any more depressing?

Of course it could. The prospect of Grove Farm looms large.

Several acres of farmland on the north bank of the Trent and overlooked by the concrete giant that is Clifton Bridge, Grove Farm was open to all elements and all park footballers every weekend with its score or more of football, rugby and hockey pitches.

Its hub was the old large farmhouse which passed for dressing rooms. Pigs wouldn't have eaten in there, though chickens clearly had been accommodated at some stage given the state and smell of its tiny compartmented myriad of dressing rooms.

The Cortina bumps and scrapes its way over half a mile of dirt track road to reach the farm gates then the car park.

Stepping out, the temperature drops by five degrees beside the river while the wind picks up to force 5. If it is meant to blow away the cobwebs, curry and ale, it isn't working.

Inside the farmhouse, Notts County A are the only team changing and get the deluxe dressing room replete with running tap water, cold only.

"Glad you could make it Rocky," Mick Walker, the youth team coach who knows my social habits, is tending his flock.

Smithy and myself are the only professionals in the side, one apprentice and the rest are schoolboys. Up the tight staircase for a swift weight loss of chicken madras I notice a poppadum has also descended into the equation. Strange, can't recall ordering any side dishes. Downstairs 10 minutes before kick-off and Walker gives his motivational team talk. I attempt to stifle my volcanic posterior surveying the dressing room. It could be an audition to cast the Von Trapp family in a *Sound of Music* remake. And that includes Brigitta, Marta and the angelic Gretl.

Christ, this lot should not be let out unless under parental supervision. Fortunately their mums and dads are outside on the touchline at No.1 pitch awaiting their little cherubs, which is the pitch nearest the Trent and more exposed to the gust that is, worryingly, picking up considerably. On one of his good days, a Stubbs volley would easily traverse the river in this sort of howling torrent.

Smithy and nine fresh-faced, so-enthusiastic-it-hurts, youngsters run out on No.1 pitch with two substitutes who should have been in nursery having a bottle of milk and a mid-morning nap at this time of day. Followed by a bleary-eyed, unshaven wretch reeking of chicken curry. Welcome Captain Madras.

Pondering my fate, I am alerted to the lack of opposition warming up in the other half of the pitch, which is a mudheap with dangerously iced and rutted penalty areas. Perhaps it has been called off. Please.

Fat chance. Nottingham Forest A duly arrive over the horizon in the plush, heating-controlled, first-team coach that reverses up as near as it can to the playing area before parking, coming to rest sedately as if a spaceship from another galaxy had just parked on a medieval cow pat for a close encounter of the turd kind.

Bit posh for a batch of young wannabees. I am bemused. Not for long. Unlike Lowry-style matchstick men aliens, Forest emerge in Indian file and pristine Garibaldi red shirts and white shorts. From the bowels of their luxurious coach there came luxurious players.

David Needham, formerly of County and a Championship winner the previous season, John O'Hare, two titles with Derby and Forest, Ian Bowyer, title winner. The impressive list went on impressively. With their game also abandoned, Clough has sent a side of first-teamers. "Eyup Davie boy, what the fuck are you doing here?" asked my former County colleague Needham.

"I could ask you the same fucking question Neddy."

"No idea son. Gaffer wants us all to get some match practice. You're a clever lad, Ours not to reason why..."

"...their's but to do and die."

It was just plain unfair. Did Jimmy know? Was this some sort of sick conspiracy?

Joe Frazier climbing into the ring with Jimmy Osmond was on a par with this mismatch though in fairness the long-haired lover from Scouseland would deserve everything Big Joe threw at him.

Surely there would be a stewards' inquiry.

I am walking to the centre circle to toss a coin and fail to notice the last player to exit the team coach.

"Bollocks! I am going to die," as Britain's first £1million player jogs past on my way back to lining up at centre -half. "Fucking death by slow, methodical, football torture." As the garam masala takes more of a hold, men on grassy knolls and lunar moon walkers with flapping flags enter the conspiracy conundrums that are unfolding here.

With the wind at their backs, Forest immediately attack before a wayward effort sails over the bar and strikes the Starship Nottingham Forest coach, much to the chagrin of its first officer trying to snatch a hot cup of coffee from his thermos flask on the bridge. On retrieving the ball, the young County goalkeeper steadies himself for the first goal kick.

I gaze at him. I want to offer encouragement. What the fuck is his name?

I had been introduced to all the novices before kick-off but with a raging hangover the introductions were lost on me. His name was Tom. Little Tom. Or Tim. Tiny Tim. Could have been Tammy Wynette for all I knew or cared. Just kick the fucking thing son.

Giving it his mightiest punt, the ball gains altitude around the 18-yard box where it hits turbulence that forces it back into the area to Francis who tries to pounce before the referee blows for a re-take.

"Sorry Trevor, but it's not in play technically," advises the man in the black. The second attempt doesn't make it out of the box either. Time for Captain Madras to step up to the plate.

In the frozen sludge against the wind, I just cleared the penalty area where Forest regain possession. To Francis who runs at and past me as if I wasn't there, which was precisely what I was wishing at that moment.

Still, I manage to breathe heavily on the million pound man, doubtless instrumental in him slicing his shot wide of the target, that and the rutted divots that might have broken an ankle with the wrong footing.

Consummate professional that he is, Francis does not complain about the surface or the state of Captain Madras' curry-induced halitosis.

Clough and his managerial partner Peter Taylor then appear on the touchline, barking orders, encouraging and dismantling egos in equal measure.

Francis again, so lively and nimble, runs at defenders, young hopefuls who were playing for Mundella or Ellis Guilford Secondary School the previous week.

He is a class apart. County A are classrooms apart.

I can only admire his pace, control and poise. *Wonder if he thinks the same about me?*

The closer I get tight to mark my man, the further Francis moves away. And away from goal. The curry breath is working its magic.

Garlic and garam masala, what a pair. But where had that poppadum come from?

Astonishingly, the black and white stripes begin to find some confidence, Smithy running about like the clappers performing the role of two players, which is a necessity today.

By half-time, it is 2-0 to County Under-10s. Smokin' Joe is on the ropes. Little Jimmy is bobbing and weaving.

"This can't go on Mick," I look incredulous at the coach.

"Just go with it Rocky. They're playing well aren't they?"

"Bloody fantastic lads. You're a credit to yourselves and your parents here. And don't worry about that nippy little bugger up front. He's in my pocket."

After an hour, the curry breath has worn off. Francis polishes off a flowing move then an equaliser and the million pound man is substituted. Clough and Taylor have seen enough and substitute themselves to the warmth of their homes or Ladbrokes.

It could have been many more but Tiny Tim or Tammy Wynette, I never did get to find out his name, now with the wind at his back but still having difficulty launching his goal kicks on an escape trajectory from the penalty area, produces several remarkable saves. It is 2-2 at the final whistle.

Handshakes all round. Great thrill for the young lads, great relief for me.

Surreal does not even get close as a description.

Forest are beamed back to planet City Ground.

Back to the pub for yours truly. Back to the crèche for my team-mates.

February 16

NO game tomorrow, called off again as are most of the matches. Another trip for the reserves to Hyson Green Boys Club, courtesy of McVay's Transit Vans. A level of proficiency leads me to believe that Jimmy must be grooming me for Jolly Jack's sub chauffeur or life in a green shirt and jacket driving the city's Corpo double-deckers backwards and forwards over Clifton Bridge to the land of my raising. Given the heater is turbo-charged in this Ford, I consider taking it home and sleeping overnight in preference to the flat which once more has turned into an icebox. Frozen solid like its inhabitants.

February 22

A RETURN to the grass at Wilford Tip and the sound of Jimmy's whistle echoes around the bin lorries in the moist morning air. And then there is the oft repeated 'DK, DK Archie boy' or 'DK, DK Vint son' as the practice match marches relentlessly to the tune of a sporadic Sirrel-tooting interruption. Apart from the top 100 players he has faced or played with (we are down to No.59 and in Lenny Glover territory when the court of Jeff Blockley is in session), he has brought the phrase DK with him. At first amusing, fairly encouraging, it's now a grating sore that sends Jack's fearless scalpel running for cover. Maybe it's because I never seem to be the recipient of the Blockers approval. Perhaps he could throw me one now and again as a bone to a dog to keep me quiet. And happy. Surely we are all Different (K)Class in our own way.

March 5

SOME of the Hope Drive intellectuals have persuaded me to pay and see *The Deer Hunter* at the ABC up Chapel Bar as a birthday treat. Reminded so much of that game at Orient which lasted 89 minutes too long only this endured three hours and three minutes overtime just to hear *God Bless America*. On reflection Brisbane Road offered the better deal even without the Russian roulette.

March 10

ARCHIE Mann scores in the dying minutes at Cambridge. A few seconds later Jimmy shunts me on. My first win bonus since Titanic sank. You beauty Arthur. £80 for 60 seconds sweat and toil, nice work if you can get it. Celebrate with Pedro and Smithy in the TBI and Flyer but head back to flat before Tiffany's, a kind of torture chamber on several levels that passes for a disco. Thinking more about getting away from Nottingham and County. Killer, through the Sirrel diaries and scribbled jottings, has already told me York and Peterborough have been making enquiries.

March 15

THE morning I started pre-season training at Notts County was the day after my schooldays ended at Fairham Comp for Boys. The following new term, it went mixed, at least in the sixth form, for the first time in its history. Young girls through the front gates and women teachers turning up in the staff car park. The story of my repressed adolescent life, I used to laugh. Nervously. Now on the way out of Meadow Lane, the County 75 lottery office is well and truly established where members of the opposite sex are a daily lure to post-training activities, Smithy and Pedro leading moths-like to the flame when day is done around noon or 12.30. Still when the alternative is extra laps or doggies on the pitch or another circuit in the weights room-groundsman's storage unit under the main stand where Peter keeps his compost mix, there really is no competition.

March 19

IN the almost empty first-team dressing room Jack Wheeler was relating, as always in hushed tones, a conversation with Jimmy earlier that day. He had suspected he would be greeted by the boss for an early morning de-briefing whilst he bathed after being told on Friday he was heading north of the border to watch potential talent in the Highland Leagues.

"Jesus Jackson, those boys just keep playing football, eh!"

"You mean the Forest boss?"

"I do Jackson. Geez whizz, eh."

Sluggish and seemingly beaten and 1-0 down at half-time on Saturday, Forest recovered and romped to a 3-2 win over Southampton to retain the League Cup at Wembley.

"They tell me yer man across the water had a free bar for the players the night before. Jesus Jackson, that would never do, eh?"

"Seemed to work for them boss," Jack knew he was venturing into dangerously controversial territory and his hushed tones became an almost silent whisper as he continued his journey into the unknown.

"Aye, aye, Jackson, not a bit of it." Jack knew Sirrel would not, could not, be contradicted.

"But they won boss."

"Aye, and you know how Jackson. Do you fucking know how?"

"How's that boss?" Jack was now back to playing the game with Jimmy.

"Because they just keep playing football. Take away the goalkeeper and you could buy the rest for a slice of pizza at yer man's restaurant in town."

"Maybe boss."

"But he keeps telling them to pass that football, Jackson. And by fucking christ they fucking pass that fucking ball, eh. Birtles to Woodcock to McGovern to O'Neill.

"It's good to watch isn't it boss?"

"Jesus Jackson, am no interested in pretty, pr-ett-y, football," Sirrel was spitting out the word in contemptuous fashion.

"It's the result Jackson. It's a simple game Jackson, eh. You know who complicates it?"

"Who's that boss?" Wheeler asked already well aware of the answer.

"The fucking players Jackson, eh son. And the coaches who want to tweak this and twizzel that, eh. But those boys, they just keep it simple. Aye, he has something yer man over there."

"Seems so boss."

A slight pause encouraged Wheeler that there endeth the lesson and he departed the bathroom where Sirrel was engaging the tank-issue carbolic for cleansing purposes.

Jack had much to endure but he did it all with a smile and time for us lads. Like he had a bit of love for us all. It was mutual.

March 24

TEN minutes on for Vinter at Cold Blow Lane and another win bonus. Milwall 0, O'Brien free-kick 1. Jimmy never names me substitute for home games, Benjy seems to get the nod for that one, but always takes me away to sit on the bench. Must be something to do with my winning smile and entertaining conversation.

Supersub David Fairclough I am most certainly not yet there is such an element of superstition in the game. Last out of the dressing room, left or right boot on first, which useless effing sub will make the difference today. Two brief encounters and four points mean it's me for now as far away from Meadow Lane as possible. For the best. For both player and fans.

March 29

A MIDWEEK win over Cardiff has given us a squeak of a chance at promotion. Jimmy has called a meeting to discuss battle plans in the first-team dressing room, rammed to the rafters with the entire squad, apprentices included. The air of expectation before training builds steadily, awaiting the double swing doors to open with a whoosh as Jimmy bursts through in his thoroughly oversized and ill-fitting baggy black shorts and blue tracksuit top. Churchill or Monty addressing the troops. Apt since the first-team will be fighting them on the sand-pit of a beach that is the Goldstone Ground this Saturday, newly-signed Martin Chivers and all. Smithy decides to ease the tension and slides the length of the oblong formica-topped table that sits in the middle of the dressing room. Arriving at the far end to his baying audience, he lets rip a raspberry of truly cosmic intensity cultivated somewhere between the Star of India on Arkwright Street and Shippos Red Star Brewery at Basford with a hint of barbecued spare ribs from the Oriental Pearl, Sherwood Rise thrown in.

Seconds later, the generalissimo arrives to a nasal assault akin to nerve gas in the Verdun trenches.

"Jesus fucking christ, David," Jimmy seems to have identified the joker despite the diminutive card being shuffled back in his rightful place at the back of the pack.

"All this just to massage your ego and enhance your reputation, eh son?" he continues, tut-tutting.

There is a brief silence. Jimmy is looking at me. The entire dressing room follows suits and sniggers. Smithy, partially hidden, is laughing uncontrollably, winking at me.

It is pointless to argue. Surely the gaffer knows I'm a Home Ales man and never touch a chinky? No matter, no chance of a Brighton win bonus. Bugger Brighton. And fuck your smart arse Smithy.

April 4

DREAMS of Clifton, JFK and Fat Man on a Beach, a programme on telly some years ago which I saw at 19 Listowel late at night. The title accurately summed it up. Resonated with me then. Still does. Maybe it's the fat man thing that I can identify with except the fat man is dead now. Committed suicide around the same time as Nick Drake. And the meaning is McVay?

April 7

Dave Bury hosts another party. I invite other friends to sample his vodka and terrace. Fish, Marshall, Watson, Hammond and Booth. Sounds like the crew of a fated Polar expedition, the sort that Ladybird books once glorified and I'd read during school lessons at Milford Juniors. The gallant explorers, the stiff Upper Lips, the four-legged friends left behind and then the tragedy of heroic failure in frozen, barren wastes. Today sad to say, doing a Captain Oates is just a euphemism for wandering off rambling drunk into the night on a solo mission to discover a toilet or park bench not a selfless sacrifice to save fellow humans in distress. And now come to think of it, why were all those grown-up blokes snuggling up in the privacy of their pint-sized tent in splendid isolation? Not that this lot of degenerates from Fairham Comp are beacons of respectability. Paul is not amused. By 5am it is too late. The vodka has dried up. The terrace remains intact. Sunday is a good day to sleep it off and snuggle up among the milk bottles on my own balcony. I have an empathy with milk bottles, empty or full, Ronnie would agree.

April 14

IT has been a disastrous week for the promotion push. A thrashing at Sheffield United then two games in two days over Easter yielding just a point at home to Oldham after a Bad Friday defeat to Sunderland where Ricky Green was given half an hour as a substitute to rescue the 3-0 deficit. No surprise he failed. He's not had the rub of his own name since signing and as much as he has everyone's empathy, he will be better for a move onwards and downwards where he can regain his confidence. It's been shattered here at Meadow Lane, a fish out of water for a really good pro and decent sort. He's just not Les Bradd and worse he knows it. A goal, at any level, will be a welcome relief for Ricky.

April 18

THAT old David Fairclough supersub magic is back. A few minutes longer to earn the bonus but well deserved with a 2-1 win over Newcastle in front of just over 12,000 distinctly pissed-off Geordie fans. This was the game that was called off the day Francis made his debut for Forest A at Grove Farm but the extra money tonight was tinged with regrets, namely a League Cup exit three years ago. So much is coming back near the end of my time at the Lane to aggravate and annoy. After a sequence that had seen Sunderland, Leeds and Everton ousted, we had been confident going to St James' Park. Or I was until Ronnie told me to play outside right in a 4-4-2 on the morning of the game. Shock tactics and I was unable to respond in kind. Soaking now in St James' Olympic-size communal bath and thinking (Jacques Cousteau prepared for his dives here and it's in these depths that they filmed the giant squid grappling scenes for *Voyage to the Bottom of the Sea* as Richard Basehart and David Hedison staggered up and down the set of the Seaview like demented drunks on the Palais revolving dance floor). Thinking that I was charging about in not too dissimilar headless chicken circles trying to cope with Alan Kennedy at left-back. Of course Malcolm Macdonald's long throw fisted in by Eric Mac won the tie but for me, the Wembley dream ended somewhere between the first and fifth minute, a self-inflicted psychological warfare that was only going to finish with a white flag raised in the right-winger's camp.

Naturally I blamed Ronnie at the time or anyone in close proximity for my failure to turn up at the ground. But really down to me. Could do better. By coincidence it was a recurring theme on my school reports.

Kneeling to avoid the risk of high winds, Iain McCulloch, the Cat, poses for the pre-season cameras before flying off to Toton.

April 18

THE numbers game absorbs the grey matter tonight. Perched sixth just three rungs below a promotion place, it might have been a handy position to be but for a goal difference resembling an Arctic thermometer, minus two and counting. The notion of going up to the highest level had been a fanciful one for some time.

The tables can lie Jimmy.

Still, as that occasional No.12, I have reaped the occasional reward of bonuses that come with keeping the bench snug while enduring all that Jimmy's right hand could inflict on left or right thigh during the course of 90 frenetic minutes. On reflection, bonuses were merited as danger money alone.

If I felt any guilt at all, it had dissipated in the Arriba after last night's victory as the extra cash was being put to good use in that darkened den of a death trap, more so as *Baker Street* weaved its haunting sax solo from the top floor disco. If ever I unwittingly paid to get in, god preserve us, it would be worth the entrance fee alone to hear it.

"Thing is, there are some blokes who'll turn up at a party with a Bowie or Carole King LP under their arm and swear blind that they are into that kind of music," Benjamin was uncharacteristically aggressive about covert come-to-bed tactics.

"Benjy, I'd take the Bay City Rollers Greatest Hits as long as it interested the chicks, know what I mean my son?"

"Chicks? Chicks Smithy!! It's nearly 1980 pal." Benjy compelled to represent sister chicks everywhere.

"It's all the same as long you get to weigh-hey a few jugs before midnight."

Religion and politics were never a threat to intellectual fall-outs after midnight up Bottle Lane.

"Ey up, there's old Statler and Waldorf over there," Benjy was changing direction and subject as Sammy Chapman and Billy Brindley moved to a corner discussing the meaning of football, more pressing than matters of life or death according to a certain northern football manager.

I had to admire the two of them, Brindley playing part-time locally with his 'proper job' now he had finished at Gillingham. Apprentices together at Forest, indomitable characters on and off the pitch, it was their passion for the game that I at once admired but also loathed. How can anyone be so obsessed with a fucking game? On the other side, Brindley's indifference to authority, his ability to cajole, coax and entice laughter in even the bleakest of souls. How could you resist that?

Please don't turn into the Muppet Show, the mind and body was swaying to a surplus of gin and Roxy Music's *Dance Away*.

Two hours later, I was rendering a fair impression of the muppets on the settee, smashing the cardboard box dining table that passed for Steve Upton's drum kit with a knife and fork. *Time Was* and Wishbone Ash never sounded so reassuringly hollow.

April 26

A MASS exodus is predicted during the summer; McManus, Mann, Vinter all want away for better things or better money. I just want away and the insular football bush telegraph revealed that Peterborough were now favourites to make a bid. Even Lincoln City entered into the reckoning. Perhaps the Smurf had forgiven my deplorable impersonation of a professional footballer in that County Cup debacle at Field Mill a year ago. Who could tell but it confirmed that the world was my oyster providing it was residing on football's sea bed, 20,000 leagues down below the rarefied air of the First Division.

Whatever or whoever was trawling those depths in search of a club or player come the end of the season, a Jap sub had surfaced earlier this month from the murky waters onto a City Ground quagmire to deter Clough and Taylor's European Cup progress.

The man from the land of the rising sun was named Okudera, alighting from the Cologne bench late in the semi-final stages to level the scores at 3-3. With away goals counting double, the general consensus was that Forest were a busted flush for the second leg, a theory fostered by the headline in a tabloid national the following morning: *Jap Sub Sinks Forest*. Of course it didn't. Ian Bowyer's header in Germany sent Forest through to the European Cup final last night. Unbelievable.

April 30

BY a quirk of fate, a gentleman with an abundance of experience in the seamanship of the submariner, particularly in times of national conflict, loomed large in my County farewell.

Back to where it all began, here endeth the lesson. A symmetry, if less than perfect. If that is even possible grammatically or realistically.

Our last away game of the season was at Selhurst Park on Saturday but Jimmy had flitted back to his roots on yet another scouting mission, leaving Jack Wheeler in charge of the first-team.

Against all odds, I had managed to squeeze into the 16-man squad on merit but realised my chances of making an appearance were slim. Based on such irrefutable logic, I had invited the trusty County coach driver Geoff for a few drinks after our Friday evening meal.

We had shared pints together from Burton Albion to Bristol City and I enjoyed his tales of the Second World War as a crew member on a British sub. Often on the receiving end of a few ear-bashings from Jimmy, some good-natured banter, others not so, I got the impression that trying to turn a deaf ear to a Gorbals rant was small beer compared with dodging depth charges and wondering if your next breath of stale recycled air would be your last.

Since Geoff served on the submarines, accordingly he liked to sink a few, which he obliged in the nearby equivalent of the Rose and Crown though he stopped at four pints. After all, he was driving the following day. I stopped at five and three double whiskies. After all, I was doing naff all the following day.

Gentle Jack was on room patrol by 10.30 but only knocked on doors and then turned in for the night himself so when I staggered back just before midnight, the coast was all clear.

Which was more than could be said for my head at breakfast.

"Gather round you boys, the gaffer has just rang me from Scotland," Jack announced in his official voice and official role as keeper of the faith and first-team sheet in Jimmy's absence as I battled gamely with a boiled egg whose resistance to crack was getting the better of this predator's tea spoon and will to live.

"Now the team is: McManus in goal, Richards, right-back...."

And so it went on until, "...and the substitute will be McVay."

There was a smug look on Vinter's face, having spotted me lurching to my room the night before.

"Are you sure, Jack? Not misheard the boss have you?"

"David, this is the team the gaffer phoned over to me 10 minutes ago. Would I get it wrong?"

I surrendered to the boiled egg and went back to bed to sleep or better still throw up. On the team coach to the match, I was trying to focus on the players, recalling my debut at the same venue six years previously, playing poker on the trip to Crystal Palace's ground with a deck of circular cards Pat and Aunty Peggy had bought me when working for J.H. Bell Stationers on Pelham Street. A mind full of meaningless trivia has always been my burden to bear.

"I've never played with round cards before," Stubbs, sitting opposite at the card table, had remarked.

"I've never played at Selhurst Park," I replied.

"Neither have I son."

It certainly was a step up for nearly every County player, a pristine stadium at a club relegated from the First Division just a few months earlier. Hammond, he of the Clumber Street public house run, was present to greet friends from Nottingham having recently been promoted to first choice goalkeeper at Selhurst Park.

Malcolm Allison was manager then. Now an equally flamboyant cockney in Terry Venables was trying to push Palace back into the top division after that fall from grace.

Big Stubbs and Vinter, scorers on that day, Mann and Masson as well, were still at the club but Roy Brown, Brindley, Worthington, Probert and Randall, all gone from that sweltering August afternoon.

Six years on and this was a new order on the bus. Hooks, Hunt and of course Mair, in my wayward mind the young lad I had mentored in Magaluf. In what? Car roof hopping? St Miguel sloshing?

"Come on McVay, time to wake up, kicking off soon you know," Vinter was poking me in the chest. "Do you want some headache tablets son?"

"Fuck off Vint."

One down after five minutes, Stubbs and Blockley hold firm until the former lunges for a loose pass.

"Christ, I think he's pulled something," Jack concerned in the away-team dugout.

"Do you think so Jack? Really?" me ditto in ditto.

"Go and get warmed up David. It's nearly half-time, you'll have to go on for the big man in the second half son."

"Do you think so Jack? Really?"

Forty minutes later, I am still trying to catch Vince Hilaire who is sentencing anyone in his path to death by nutmeg. I am severely punished, on the one hand trying to stop the budding talent while on the other trying to count and recall if I'd really had a third double scotch for a nightcap in the Rose and Crown.

Masson looks round unimpressed, as if asking himself what has he let himself in for…fair comment.

Red of face, devoid of breath, I catch myself (at least I could do that since Hilaire was out of the question) scanning the men in the yellow kit. McCulloch, Hooks, Hunt; Pedro and O'Brien at full-backs. DK as Blockers would say. But not me. This was the County tomorrow; I was yesterday's man.

Arthur Mann, switched to centre-half, has words of comfort, as always.

"Doing a great job Rocky, keep going my son," he urges while Masson's glare indicates a contrary assessment, something along the lines of 'you fucking useless tosser'.

He has a point. Palace have two when Jerry Murphy adds a second late on and they remain on the brink of going up.

"David can I have a few words?" Terry Bowles asked me as I stumbled out of the dressing room door. "What me Terry?" knowing as any self-respecting hack would that I was old news at Meadow Lane.

"Just trying to get a few features piled up for the new publication."

"What's that?"

"*Nottingham News*, first edition came out last week. We've got Cloughie on board, he's stopped talking to the *Evening Post*.

"Well so will I mate if it helps, though I doubt it will. Workers unite and all that is it?"

"The 28 they wouldn't take back have started it, yes."

"Good for you ...and them. But you know I'm on the way out here, don't you Terry?"

"Peterborough isn't it?"

"You tell me. Players usually the last to know. But Archie Mann and Vint will be going I reckon. And Eric Mac."

"I can get them later."

"Meaning I might not be around the first-team from now on."

"Meaning you might prove somewhat elusive David on match days until the end of the season."

"Like that fucking whippet Hilaire!"

"He's a handful."

"Sober or otherwise."

"Pardon."

"Look Terry, happy to do a piece. Just don't mention last night's pre-match evening meal."

"A liquid diet?"

"A Kenwood Chef at the beer pumps and the top shelf combined."

"You never learn."

"And what odds were there on the boss picking me today? I reckon the air up in Jockland loosens a few screws of his."

"So what are your plans now?"

"I think I'm ready to tackle a drink."

"Be your first tackle of the day then."

"Thanks Terry. When did you say you wanted to interview me?"

"Not a good time now, clearly. Meet you at the ground on Monday lunchtime?"

"Are you allowed in and all that?"

"Listen we're the members of the NUJ mate. It's the little shithouses that the *Post* keep sending down who aren't. But they will all be blacked. All of them, take my word for it."

"I will Terry. Good luck. See you Monday."

Bowles' appearance had focused my mind in search of the players' bar. Don't even know the name of Peterborough's manager. But yes, moving on was the only real option.

I got to rearrange my life, I got to rearrange my world. Bloody hell, Ted and Martin Turner were revealing my kismet on *Argus*, I was grasping for air and some reality.

Wishbone Ash echoing beneath the Selhurst Park main stand was freaking me out. Seriously so. In a sweat.

Almost as much as giving chase to that bastard Hilaire down the touchline, forcing him towards O'Brien before the sneaky little sod nipped between the two of the us, two fingers up as he passed effortlessly by. Double bastard!

Still sweat was good. The last of the branded scotch was filtering through the system. Future uncertain, of that I am sure. Destination undefined.

Somewhere different. Somewhere that did not require an Anglo-Scottish translator at team meetings.

Wishbone Ash still resonated around the rafters when I spotted a sign for the players' suite.

Time for a change. Time for a drink. Plumping for the Australian lager instead of the Holsten Pils. Something different. Baby steps. No need to be radical and rush things.

Gaduated from Mackeson and stout to San Miguel and First Division football but Gordon Mair was helped by some twinkled-toed skills honed on Majorcan car roofs.

May 1

LESS than 4,500 turn out to see a 1-1 draw with Wrexham. Pitiful in every sense. Stubbsy, cause of all my problems on Saturday afternoon after 3.45, has made an instant recovery. Why couldn't he have done that at the weekend?

May 2

RESEARCH tells me that Peter Morris is manager at Peterborough, the daft bugger who tried to sign me at Mansfield. Small world, football. Well not so much research as he rang me at the ground today. Still no phone at the flat (deliberately so) it's the only means of direct contact. The Posh boss wants to meet in the summer before I head off on holiday. Following the route from Meadow Lane to Fenlands taken by Mick Jones and Jon Nixon. Hush hush at the moment, he informs me. I have news for him.

May 4

FRIDAY is Jolly Jack's visit to the club to pay the wages and sort things out. And my how jolly he is this morning. And why not? He's returned as a Labour MP in his local constituency and Maggie is in power in Downing Street after yesterday's General Election. A Tory government and a Tory in red clothing and red tie in Nottingham East. Jack was never so jolly.

Should have voted but what the hell, a vote against the chairman only meant one for Martin Brandon-Bravo. Unimaginable, unforgiveable. If it were possible, Granddad would have disowned me from up on high if I had voted for that double-barrelled Tory twat.

This is my final day at the Lane, no point in prolonging the agony. Though not many appear to share my despondency. Dennis Marshall, positively beaming, hands me my last wage packet, the small brown envelope no longer with cash enclosed but a proper pay slip with taxes and totals written on a thin transparent material resembling Greeny's Izal bog paper issue at the Newmarket. Something fitting there, wages and their inevitable destination. Jolly Jack is even on the premises, making sure I leave in an orderly fashion no doubt. The glasses, teeth and that permanent smile. Glad to see the back of me. In fact everybody is so happy to see me fucking well go! Still, the chairman is getting some sort of fee I am sure which, given fines re-invested in the club, probably adds up to a tidy profit. Even a last sneak at Maud's pride and joy spin-dryer in the wash room gets a laugh from Albert.

"You leaving son?"

"The tea will never be the same Albert."

"Good luck lad."

It's a fragmented farewell. Most of the senior pros have buggered off after Saturday with no County Cup to detain them. One or two apprentices. That is the football way. No long, lingering goodbyes. Grab your boots and off you go. You know the day will come, the writing on the wall and all that but you never prepare, no long-term plans just wait for the next contract. Should one be offered and that is not always the case.

Part of me yearns for another night at Elland Road, another cup win over Leeds or Everton and Sirrel's earnest and animated approbation.

But that is the past. Fleeting. Soon forgotten. Football moves on quickly, taking no prisoners, as Jimmy told Killer, leaving just stragglers.

Besides it's craving a yesterday, like the Morecambe and Wise Christmas, that didn't exist quite so wonderfully as I recall it, inspired by a mixture of gin and Nick Drake to create the blurred but always mellow memory of a past perfect.

"Game's gone," is the best of Brindley's philosophy. But he knows like me it's always going to be there. Part of you. More so him than me, truthfully.

Jimmy emerges from his office on the sloping car park area outside the Main Stand. "I wish you well, eh David. You did a good job for me eh son," he ventures before heading off in full training kit to put the apprentices through their paces. Poor bastards. But then enriched by his tutoring in so many ways.

Sirrel the fixture; me and the other players the fittings, temporary to be sure.

When you said 'good job' I think for once you were at the wrong game boss.

After the symmetry of the Palace goodbye, Stoke win and were promoted at Meadow Lane last Saturday. It's a year almost to the day since that match at the Victoria Ground ensured we were safe. As a parting gift it's not much, but it's the best I can offer.

** Despite advice to the contrary, Posh manager Peter Morris did sign me for all of £25,000 that summer of 1979. At the end of May, having graduated from his A team debut to his European one for the club, Trevor Francis headed the winning goal for Nottingham Forest to secure the European Cup for Clough and Taylor's Forest against Malmo in Munich. By then, the pigs were feeding on left-over madras and poppadum in the desolate home-team dressing room at Grove Farm. Truly, funny how things work out.

Still further Round the Bend beyond Meadow Lane

The Management:

JIMMY SIRREL: Having departed to Sheffield United in October 1975, Jimmy made the return journey after a double-dismissal. His own at Bramall Lane and Ronnie Fenton's by chairman Jack Dunnett in October 1977. One of his first tasks was to rescue me from Torquay United, a smashing, family club, to which I had been banished on a month's loan. He then steered the club clear of the relegation zone and safety later on that season. With Howard Wilkinson, he realised his dream of taking Notts into the First Division when the side gained promotion in 1981, by strange coincidence just a couple of seasons after I left. The feat fulfilled a remarkable voyage from the nether regions of the Fourth Division, where Notts were languishing when Jimmy was appointed in 1969. He enjoyed his 80th birthday in the company of former players, friends and invited guests at Meadow Lane in February 2002 and lived in his adopted village of Burton Joyce, where he was a regular at the Cross Keys pub with another legendary Scot Dave Mackay, until his death in 2008. His funeral was held in St Mary's Church at the hub of the city's Lace Market before he was laid to rest next to his wife Cathy, who died in 1984, in the church graveyard at Burton Joyce.

JACK WHEELER: Jack went on to complete nearly 30 years' service for the Magpies, seeing them reach the old First Division with Jimmy and Howard Wilkinson in charge. When he retired, in 1985, Jack Dunnett took him into his office and offered him his thanks for giving blood, sweat and tears to the club – and a form on how to apply for disability benefit because of his dodgy hips that had become an occupational hazard sitting in wet and windy dugouts from Scunthorpe to Hartlepool via Bournemouth. He was the first to be honoured by the Former Players' Association in 2001. He lived with Olga, his wife, in the clubhouse in Wollaton, near Nottingham, that he moved into when he first came to Notts with Tommy Lawton in 1957 until his death in 2009. A memorial service for Jack was also held in St Mary's and like Jimmy's, it was crammed full of the former players, acquaintances and colleagues who cherished and revered this gentle man so dearly.

RONNIE FENTON: Even before he inherited the reigns from Jimmy in 1975 Ronnie and I never did see eye-to-eye, a frequent occurrence in the workplace never mind professional football. After two near misses at promotion, a dreadful start to the 1977-78 season saw his departure. However, his tenure was responsible for boldly going where no Notts manager had gone before, beyond Gibraltar on exotic tours to Magaluf and Kenya. He swiftly crossed the River Trent and forged a supremely successful alliance with Brian Clough at Nottingham Forest, which tells you more about his football acumen than mine. Died in 2013 aged 73.

JACK DUNNETT: Jolly Jack – the nickname is facetious – ran a tight ship at Meadow Lane but his character references left something to be desired. When he sold the club in 1987 he had already served as President of the Football League but his ambition to be similarly acclaimed in the Football Association ultimately went unfilled. Became vice-chairman of Portsmouth in 1989 but fell from grace and off the football radar shortly afterwards. Now in his nineties, lives in retirement in South London.

MICK JONES: Got to know Jonah for only a few weeks before he was shipped off to Peterborough United in the pre-season of 1973 (a route which I was to follow six years later) but he could not have been more helpful with advice and encouragement for this novice professional. He was less helpful when he returned as Ronnie's able lieutenant a few years later but since Jonah has now accumulated four different periods at Meadow Lane (one as a stalwart utility player during County's rise from the Fourth to Second Division), neutrals might suspect there is a touch of either masochism or insanity coursing through his bloodstream. A genuine man of football and football man, he remains one of the good guys whose numbers appear to be diminishing with alarming rapidity in the modern game.

SQUAD 1977-79

GOALKEEPERS:

ERIC McMANUS: A move to Stoke City when in the prime of his form did not auger well for Eric. He suffered a severe elbow injury at the Victoria Ground and moved on to Bradford City before finishing his career with Tranmere Rovers. Latterly involved in coaching with Coventry City, Derby County and Walsall.

FRANKIE LANE: The perennial understudy to Ray Clemence at Liverpool, Frankie played out a similar role to Eric McManus before his big chance came in a promotion tussle with Blackpool at Meadow Lane. Unfortunately handling errors proved costly in a 2-1 home defeat, effectively ending his County career, playing later for Kettering Town. Like most goalkeepers, thought he was Denis Law in front of goal during five-a-sides and certainly would have given Jimmy Greaves in his pomp a run for his lager in front of the bar. Died in 2011, aged just 62.

COLIN KING: Even further down the net-minding pecking order than Frankie, he never really got an opportunity to shine at Meadow Lane with firstly Eric Mac in such supreme form during his last season with Notts who then signed the gentleman netminder from Yugoslavia Raddy Avramovic who became firmly established as a strong contender as the club's finest No.1. The arrival of Mick Leonard from Halifax consigned him to County history, a League Cup defeat at Grimsby his solitary senior appearance.

DEFENCE:

PEDRO RICHARDS: After ten years' service with the club, Pedro was granted a testimonial season which, considering that the Notts side was in considerable decline at the time, was not able to fulfil expectations. Rather like Pedro's own playing career. A talent that never reached its true potential. He remained in the Meadows to which he came as young Spanish-speaking schoolboy aged 11 until his untimely death aged 45, at Christmas 2001.

SAMMY CHAPMAN: Needs no introduction to Nottingham football fans. A City Ground apprentice with Billy Brindley, the pair were lifelong friends bonded by their *joie de vivre*, a mutual respect and fondness for a few pints. Sammy eventually made the forbidden journey from the south to north bank of the Trent for a brief interlude in what was a long and successful career in the game, including some memorable FA Cup exploits at Shrewsbury Town. Still to be seen flitting around village pubs from Gotham to Glapton and beyond.

JEFF BLOCKLEY: The man who put the DK into different class, Blockers certainly had a pedigree to match his dressing and hotel room stories of how he rubbed shoulders with the game's biggest names. Though he talked a magnificent game, strangely avoided the coaching or managerial career route option and went on to own his own business after a short spell at Enderby Town.

BRIAN STUBBS: Stubbsy never did move away from Meadow Lane even though many First Division managers cast an eye over his central defensive partnership with Needham. Was part of the squad that secured the Sirrel dream of taking the club from the bottom of the Fourth Division to the First. However, when Notts arrived there in 1981 he was denied his moment of glory and an appearance in the top flight by the management duo who refused to pick him despite his outstanding service. Another character who is welcomed back with open arms and ear plugs at Meadow Lane on match days. Still socializes and throws the odd dart in public houses south of the River Trent.

TRISTAN BENJAMIN: Benjy's hair blossomed far more freely than his conversation but the quiet man of Meadow Lane emerged as one of the most consistent defenders as the club secured promotion to the First Division. One of several brothers with a fine footballing tradition, he played briefly for Chesterfield before finishing in the game. Remains as reclusive and elusive as he was a conversationalist and fleet-of-foot player. Always sported a decent car when he turned pro, from a pristine Ford Cortina Mark II 1600E to a Triumph Stag whose previous owner seemed to have rodgered it to death in a case of mistaken identity. Still that love of driving perhaps lingers while apparently he works on the buses for Nottingham City Transport.

BRIAN KILCLINE: Truly a gentle giant of a young lad and now grown man who still blames me, among others, for nurturing some of his more eccentric drinking habits at a tender age. Filling the considerable hole left by Brian Stubbs when he was exiled from the first-team during Howard Wilkinson's top-flight reign, Killer was rewarded with England Under-21 caps and rave reviews until he fell foul of the nightclub culture prevalent in Nottingham in the 1980s. His transfer to Coventry City was almost an epiphany, appointed captain of the team in which capacity he lifted the FA Cup for the Sky Blues after a historic victory over Tottenham Hotspur in 1987. Spends his time over here or abroad where he has a property in Portugal with his partner Lynn.

RAY O'BRIEN: Became a part of the County folklore with his left-footed free-kicks and indecipherable accent. Lived and worked in the county while at one stage helping to manage Arnold Town, a local non-league side, along with Brindley.

MIDFIELD:

STEVE CARTER: They finally did get Carter in the film, on a remote desolate beach in the North East, the sort of environment Flash would never be caught in, dead or alive, in fact any surface north of Meadow Lane in inclement weather was pretty much anathema to his right-wing tendencies. Continued to 'corkscrew' full-backs from that berth for Derby County and Bournemouth. Later returned to Great Yarmouth to run the family whelk stall, allegedly.

DAVID HUNT: It's a little-known story that Hunt the Hunk, as his female admirers knew him, nearly cost me my job at the *Nottingham Evening Post* before it had scarcely begun when he failed to turn up for his scheduled wedding day and I failed to report it, even though I had the inside story. Whether my survival was good or bad news for journalism is a matter of some debate but I have since forgiven him. Not sure if the same applies to the jilted bride at what was termed by the red-top newspaper which published the story as a 'society wedding', surely an oxymoron, in Leicestershire. Besides, I took the view that I hadn't taken up the noble profession of sports journalism to report on the tittle-tattle and private lives of football players. That was not the way ahead for the printed word. How wrong can you be?

DAVE SMITH: His move to Torquay United signalled the end for Mike Green, the manager who took me on loan there. Mike, one of the nicest blokes in football, never stood a chance once Smithy and his underpants hit Plainmoor. Remained on the south coast in the pub trade and later branched out to nearby Plymouth where he still lives with his family. He has his chance to present his version of events at Meadow Lane in Paul Mace's book, *One Flew Over the Magpies Nest*. Worth the entrance fee.

GORDON MAIR: The more bottles of Mackeson Gordie drank as an apprentice to pile on the pounds to his fragile physique, the more he seemed to shed them, *The Invisible Man* meets *The Incredible Shrinking Man*. Fortunately, an antidote arrived just in time, pints of lager and Burger King. Or something like that. Mackeson's loss was County's gain, his creative part and finish in a memorable televised one-touch goal against Ipswich Town in the First Division being one of his finest contributions among many for the Magpies.

DON MASSON: With good reason, Masson is regarded as the greatest County player of all time, certainly by a generation who cannot recall Tommy Lawton's heady days at the club. Playing for Scotland in the 1978 World Cup Finals was perhaps his finest hour. Admits he is a changed person from his off-days as Masson the Miserable in the County dressing room. The beers were free during meetings of former players convened regularly at the Gallery Hotel he owned near Trent Bridge in the formative years of the old boys' association. Now owns an award-winning bed and breakfast establishment in the village of Elton with his second wife Brenda and is involved heavily with the Former Players' Association.

LLOYD RICHARDS: Dark yet anything but moody, Lloyd was a Derby lad with an abundance of talent who never quite made the significant breakthrough his ability merited. On our two-week tour of Kenya in 1976 and travelling back from Mombasa to Nairobi in a single decker bus rejected by Camms Collapsibles on account of its unreliability, we stopped overnight at an idyllic game lodge in the mountains to watch and hear the wildebeest rampage across the vast gloomy plains and view from close quarters rhinoceroses, giraffes and more of Mother Nature's creatures drink from an illuminated pool beneath an open veranda. As we waited in silent awe for another magnificent beast to approach the floodlit watering hole, a solitary voice whispered in my ear. "Where's the disco in this place, Macca?" Satisfactory answer, there came none.

ALAN BIRCHENALL: Long before the notorious hair-dryer treatment administered by Alex Ferguson and the revelation that planet Earth was warming up a tad too rapidly, the Birch was inflicting ridiculously heated air on dressing rooms around the nation while ripping holes far larger in the ozone layer than several hundred flocks of incontinent sheep could ever conjure up. Much-travelled with a genuine Nottingham connection, his legs were on the brink but his tales of life in the big time from London to Leicester and America captivated audiences during the tedium of training or a night out at the Arriba. The legs have totally gone now but apparently he still completes near-marathons for charitable causes as club ambassador at a ground not a million miles away from Filbert Street. The suspicion is he's running on hot air.

Dropped names like confetti but never dandruff from his golden locks, Alan Birchenall, aka the Birch, became a legend in his own hairdryer and remains one today.

ERIC PROBERT: Probey eventually left Notts in the mid-1970s with a flock of albatrosses (or whatever a group of the gathered same is called) hanging around his neck. He took over a pub near Boroughbridge and briefly appeared for Darlington as the decade came to a close. I paid a visit to one of the pubs he kept in the same decade but then lost touch but still it was with great sadness that we all received the news of this troubled soul's death in 2004.

ARTHUR MANN: Never really received the credit he deserved at Meadow Lane but went on, with Alan Buckley, to achieve greater things in a coaching capacity with Grimsby Town and West Bromwich Albion. When Arthur died in 1999, the result of a tragic accident with a fork-lift truck in the delivery yard of his employers, there were several football clubs represented by hundreds of players, past and present, young and old, whose lives he had touched all too briefly. A fitting tribute to a lovely bloke and, above all, a devoted family man. His wife Sandra is proud to present a golf trophy named after him at an annual event organised by the Former Players' Association, whose formation was inspired by Arthur's tragic death.

ATTACK:

LES BRADD: The Big Bomber was still scoring goals after County, mainly for Wigan Athletic, where with Larry Lloyd the former non-league club gained promotion from the old Fourth Division. In retirement, Les joined the County 75 lottery staff at Meadow Lane then became part of the Forest commercial staff. A terrific ambassador for Notts, he returned to Meadow Lane in a part-time capacity, helping co-ordinate events in the club's 150th anniversary year of 2012. He now is part of Football in the Community at Meadow Lane working tirelessly on charity work locally. His son Tim also made the move back from the City Ground to join Notts' commercial wing.

PAUL HOOKS: Useful with his fists and feet, young Hooks became an integral feature of the team that crashed the First Division party in 1981 and overstayed their welcome (at least for the teams that were relegated instead) for three years at the highest level of the English game. His goalscoring record speaks for itself though in football's hall of infamy there is a County team photograph, quite possibly doing the rounds on the gizmo freeway or whatever cyber space is called this week, with the boy from Cotgrave showing a little more of his private parts than he anticipated. Or perhaps he did. Either way, it's a collector's item but not for the faint of heart.

MICK VINTER: Sold for a club record fee of £150,000 to Wrexham. Vint continued to score goals at the Racecourse Ground and then the Manor Ground with Oxford United before he returned to the area with Mansfield Town. Was a keen supporter of the Former Players' Association but has suffered ill-health and the early onset of dementia in recent years.

IAN SCANLON: What can you say about Scan the Man? Even Alex Ferguson failed to get a grip on him, not for the want of trying either. Remains a cult figure at Meadow Lane and just about every other football outpost where he laid his hat and boots, namely Aberdeen and St Mirren. His visits were all too fleeting for sure but always memorable.

JOHN SIMS: Was a constant source of good humour in an unassuming manner in the dressing room. Well, he made me laugh anyway. The lure of the South Coast proved too much for the former Derby forward who subsequently did the Devon rounds, making the short trip from Exeter to Plymouth Argyle then Torquay where he ended up running a pub and was reunited with his old partner-in-crime Dave Smith.

RICKY GREEN: Trying to fill the shoes of Les Bradd was several steps too far for Ricky, one of the most amiable of colleagues who shrugged his shoulders and made the best of the mostly difficult time he endured at Meadow Lane, not all of it entirely of his own making. Was eventually shipped out to Scunthorpe where I think, or hope, he regained the goalscoring prowess that persuaded Notts to pay Chesterfield a then record club fee to the Spireites.

THE EGG MAN:

JOHN 'BILLY' BRINDLEY: One of the most enduring and endearing characters on the football circuit, Billy moved on to Gillingham but after two unhappy years in Kent he returned to Nottingham with his wife Katherine and two young children. He played for and managed several local semi-professional clubs when he finished playing full time but never lost his sense of humour or the role of ready raconteur. He was still falling off a bar stool, though whether or not he was singing *Great Balls of Fire* or recounting how the world could be my lobster sauce at the time I can't quite recall, when he signed me for Grantham Town, who he managed with Jon Nixon, in the wee small hours at that infamous Nottingham night club called the Arriba. I met up with Billy again when he helped run Notts Alliance side Ruddington, the village where he lived for the majority of his working life. The local church was packed to the rafters following his premature death, aged 60, in 2007.

THE WALRUS:

DAVID McBAY: Jimmy could get my name right when he felt in the mood. After Notts, I spent two intoxicating years with Peterborough United before being shown the door on a free. Colin Murphy, then manager of Lincoln City, enticed me to join him at Sincil Bank but rehabilitation came in the form of gainful employment as a sports reporter for the *Nottingham Evening Post*, taking Notts from the First Division under Larry Lloyd, to the Third, under Dick Bate. Lifeline and Jolly Jack's departure were a couple of worthy and uplifting items to the mostly glum news off the pitch. But then along came Derek Pavis…cue my departure to the Features Department. Stints with *The Times* and as a *Daily Telegraph* freelance followed as well as writing for *BackPass*, a wonderful slice of nostalgia-driven indulgence that recalls the way we were in a distant yet sometimes eerily recent football past. They have a saying in my hometown Workington: *plus ça change, plus c'est la même chose*. Not entirely sure that applies to the beautiful game.

OLD BOYS' NETWORK:

(mentioned in previous despatches)

ROY BROWN: Gradually lost his place to Eric McManus and moved to Mansfield Town before taking up a post as manager of a sports centre in Watford. Reports of his demise were premature when the *Nottingham Evening Post* published a brief story noting his passing some four decades ago. Roy rang the news desk to take issue with his recent death. Happily, he remains stood six foot tall above the ground today, living in Sussex and competing regularly in the former players' annual golf tournament.

DAVID NEEDHAM: 'Neddy' was destined for greater things with or without the flash cars which drew envious glances from many in the Meadow Lane car park. His move to Queens Park Rangers then to Nottingham Forest, where he gained England B recognition and was in their 1978 Championship winning side, vindicated Jimmy's faith in his former apprentice's ability. After the death of Arthur Mann, he was influential in fostering the spirit of the Former Players' Association and its organisation.

BOB WORTHINGTON: One of three footballing brothers, Bob left Notts and moved to Southend United with his flash BMW 2002 but has remained in touch with many of his friends and former colleagues in Nottingham. Plays a big part in the Former Players' Association. Has now returned to reside in his native West Yorkshire following a period living and working in France.

JON NIXON: Peter Stringfellow and Jack Nicklaus combined could not match his impressive club selection. Peterborough United and Shrewsbury Town were among those that followed for Nixo after Meadow Lane. Relocated and settled in Ireland from where he continues to be responsible for the database for the Former Players' Association.

KEVIN RANDALL: The Claw continued to defy age and rubber legs as a forward with Mansfield Town, with whom he managed one more promotion while bankrupting the North Notts club by his obsession with tubes of Deep Heat, the contents of which he would immerse himself in from head to toe before kick-off. "There he goes, down the Time Tunnel," colleagues opined and he would re-emerge on the pitch looking pallid (that was the Deep Heat) but running around as if his bollocks were on fire (see previous parenthesis). Achieved success with Chesterfield as assistant manager, a famous FA Cup semi-final defeat to Middlesborough in 1997 the highlight. Most recently, he is trying to pen his memoirs between scouting missions.

IAN BOLTON: After a loan spell at Lincoln City, the Bolt finally departed Meadow Lane to join Graham Taylor's Watford. His lightning pace, thunderous shot and Benson and Hedges smokescreen that followed him around Vicarage Road were part of the scenery as Taylor's team swept from the Fourth to the First Division as swiftly as the Bolt could light up twenty filter tips. After a short stint with Brentford he settled back in the Watford area working for a company which sells metal ramps and lifting equipment.

PAUL 'SAMMY' DYER: Sammy rode off into the sunset in his Bedford van, never to be seen again. Well apart from four seasons with Colchester United. Same thing, really.

EDDIE CLIFF: From Tranmere to Chicago and then back to Rochdale. That was Eddie's itinerary after Meadow Lane. Never did find out if he joined the teaching ranks. Their gain football's loss I suppose.

GEOFF COLLIER: Never did see Geoff after a trip ferrying Kevin Randall's green Mini-van to Blackpool in a previous publication and lifetime. Considering his drinking capacity and his taste in women, probably for the best.